The Americanization of Dixie

Also by John Egerton:

A MIND TO STAY HERE

HARPER'S MAGAZINE PRESS
Published in Association with Harper & Row
New York

The Americanization of Dixie:
The Southernization of America

JOHN EGERTON

"Harper's" is the registered trademark of Harper & Row, Publishers, Inc.

FIRST EDITION

Designed by Patricia Dunbar

Library of Congress Cataloging in Publication Data

Egerton, John.
    The Americanization of Dixie.
    1. Southern States—Civilization.   2.   United States
—Civilization—1970–   I.   Title.
F216.2.E34   917.5′03′4   73–18644
ISBN 0–06–122420–0

For Brooks and March, who belong to the
first generation of Americanized Southerners

Contents

Acknowledgments

Four of the chapters in this book include some material which was originally written, in somewhat different form, for the Southern Regional Council and for the following magazines: *City, The Nation, The Progressive, Race Relations Reporter, Saturday Review* and the Louisville *Courier-Journal & Times Magazine.*

So many people contributed ideas, information and inspiration to this book that a mere listing of their names would fill several pages. I have not attempted to compile such a list here. I hope it will suffice that all of them know I am grateful and indebted to them.

As far as I am concerned, [the South] is anywhere
south of the Canadian border.

> Malcolm X,
> as quoted by Alex Haley,
> *The Autobiography of Malcolm X*

. . . the South is going to die. That's
right: The South isn't going to be anymore.
We're going the way of the rest of the country.

> A Ku Klux Klansman,
> as quoted by Robert Coles,
> *Farewell to the South*

We, the earth people, have shattered our dreams,
yes; we have shattered our own lives, too, and our
world. Our biggest problem . . . is how to make
into a related whole the split pieces of the human
experience . . . how to connect our childhood with
the present and the past with the future. . . .

> Lillian Smith,
> *Killers of the Dream*

Prologue

"Am I a Southerner, Dad?"

The question is put by an eight-year-old boy to his father, a white, Anglo-Saxon, Protestant, middle-class, over-thirty, liberal, Southern writer who hunches agonizingly over the bloodless turnips on his typewriter keyboard, trying to write something about the Americanization of Dixie and the Southernization of America.

There is invitation in the question, and challenge, and threat; it can't be turned away. The man's answer is studied, thoughtful, tinged with a trace of pride and a hint of shame. It comes out . . . yes . . . and no.

The boy's face masks whatever impression the answer has made, if any. "I think I'll go see what's for supper," he says.

Every year, one of every five Americans changes addresses. The White House has annexes in San Clemente and Key

Biscayne. The Miami Dolphins are the champions of professional football. Thurgood Marshall is on the Supreme Court.
Robert Kennedy has been murdered in Los Angeles by a man
from the Middle East, Martin Luther King has been killed in
Memphis by an escaped convict from Missouri, and George
Wallace has been shot in a Washington suburb by a man from
Michigan. Richard Nixon has been elected President, reelected
almost by national acclaim, and then disgraced by revelations
of high crimes and misdemeanors in the White House. Two
black Southerners, Barbara Jordan and Andrew Young, have
been elected to Congress from districts in which blacks are a
minority. Billy Graham is the unofficial high priest and chaplain of America. School buses have been bombed in Denver
and Pontiac, white parents have vented their wrath on black
children at a school in Brooklyn, and Chinese Americans in
San Francisco have boycotted schools to protest integration.
Country music is all the rage in London and Tokyo, and even
in New York it is finding a following. There are 1,500 Holiday
Inns in the fifty states and in twenty foreign countries, and
there are about 4,000 Kentucky Fried Chicken stands and
5,000 Hertz Rent-a-Car outlets. You can buy a mobile home
with a porch and white columns—Tara on wheels—in Montgomery or Baton Rouge (or Detroit), and you can get Confederate money from a motel vending machine in Meridian,
Mississippi. Men have gone to the moon, women have gone to
work, kids have gone to Vietnam and Canada and communes.
There is a black mayor in Tuskegee, Alabama, and he has a
white wife, and he campaigned for Richard Nixon. Half of the
inmates in California prisons are black or Chicano, and two-
thirds of the prisoners in New York state are black or Puerto
Rican. Litton Industries is the biggest employer in Mississippi,
ITT has entered the political arena in the United States and
Chile, IBM is everywhere, and Macy's is on Miami Beach.
Birmingham's air pollution rivals the smog in Los Angeles.
The South has more school desegregation, more black elected

officials, and less unemployment than any other region of the country—and also lower wages, more poverty, and more murders per capita. You can go from Tampa to Detroit in about eighteen hours via interstate highway, from Atlanta to San Francisco in about four hours via jet, and from New York to a tarpaper shack in Louisiana in a split second via television.

With all that going on, it is hard to make sense to an eight-year-old who wants to know if he is a Southerner. The South is no longer simply a colony of the nation, an inferior region, a stepchild; it is now rushing to rejoin the Union, and in the process it is becoming indistinguishable from the North and East and West. The Union is meeting the South at the front door with overtures of welcome. It, too, is changing: Having failed for the first time to win at war, having found poverty and racism alive and menacing in its own house, the North (that is to say, all of the non-Southern states) has lately shown itself to be more and more like the South in the political, racial, social, and religious inclinations of its collective majority.

A friend of mine, a fellow Southerner who tends in his more optimistic moments to see the good side of this phenomenon of Americanization, is both weary and wary of the perennial attempts of some Southerners to keep alive the distinctive characteristics of the region. Old South nostalgia and New South narcissism are beginning to bore him excessively. Recalling that he has heard the South described as a history without a country, my friend says: "Now we have a country, and we are free to start a new history. It could be something special."

I want very much to believe that. It could indeed be something special. But the evidence that it is going to be is difficult to find. Far more visible and conspicuous are the examples of mistakes being repeated, of warnings being ignored, of opportunities being missed. Excessive preoccupation with the South as a separate entity *is* a bore and a diversion; but the opposite danger is in assimilation, in an amalgamation of regions that spreads and perpetuates the banal and the venal while it melts the great and valuable diversity of America into a homogenized purée.

The thesis of this book is that the Americanization of Dixie and the Southernization of America are homogenizing processes that are full of contradiction and ambiguity and paradox, but taken as a whole, they say more about fear and failure and estrangement in American society than they do about hope and achievement and reconciliation. The South and the nation are not exchanging strengths as much as they are exchanging sins; more often than not, they are sharing and spreading the worst in each other, while the best languishes and withers. There are exceptions, of course, and I have written about some of them here. But the dominant trends are unmistakable: deep divisions along race and class lines, an obsession with growth and acquisition and consumption, a headlong rush to the cities and the suburbs, diminution and waste of natural resources, institutional malfunctioning, abuse of political and economic power, increasing depersonalization, and a steady erosion of the sense of place, of community, of belonging.

This is a journalistic, not a scholarly, examination of some of those trends. The focus is contemporary rather than historical, and the approach is interpretive and subjective and occasionally personal. I make no claim to strict objectivity; if there is such a thing in journalism (or in history, for that matter), it is rare and elusive. The reader should understand that there are few if any unaltered recordings of actuality here; there are rather some selected pieces of reality, strung together and filtered through my own perceptions and prejudices. "All writing slants the way the writer leans," someone once said, "for no man is perpendicular—but some are upright." I have tried to be fair and accurate and honest in what I have written, recognizing that fairness and accuracy and honesty, like beauty, are in the eye of the beholder.

"Of books about the South there is no end," wrote V. O. Key in 1949 in the preface of his classic study, *Southern Politics.* "Nor will there be as long as the South remains the region with the most distinctive character and tradition." Key was right, of course; an unending succession of books has followed his. The South has generated enough fascination and inspiration and outrage to keep novelists and playwrights and scholars and journalists intent on it for almost two hundred years. Now the distinctive character and tradition that Key alluded to—the best of it and the worst—is changing under the influence of American homogenization. There is a hint of the change—subconscious and unintentional, perhaps—in the titles of some recent books, among them Robert Coles's *Farewell to the South* and a novel by Willie Morris called *The Last of the Southern Girls.* (Harry Ashmore had the first such title—*Epitaph for Dixie*—almost twenty years ago, and it is turning out to be prophetic, though not in the way Ashmore hoped it would be.) The title of this book follows that trend, and deliberately so: its intent is to say that for good and ill, the South is just about over as a separate and distinct place.

This won't be the last of the Southern books. The land won't disappear like Atlantis, and the people won't leave. On the contrary, there are more people now than ever, and their number is increasing, and many of them are black and white former Southerners trying to rediscover the lost sense of place. The South may die, but there will be survivors, and they will have something to say about whether we will in fact have a country, and a chance to start a new history. If the South's best qualities succumb and its worst characteristics prevail, all Americans will have cause to lament the Americanization of Dixie and the Southernization of America.

Nashville   JOHN EGERTON
August 1973

The Americanization of Dixie

Reflections on a Christening/Wake/Revival Celebrating the Birth/Death/Resurrection of the New/Old/Contemporary South

The printed program announces a "Symposium on the Contemporary South," to be held at the University of South Florida in Tampa. Five days, beginning January 9, 1972. The major topics to be discussed are "Two Decades of Human Rights," "The New Southern History," "The New Southern Politics," and "The South Tomorrow." The program also lists the symposium participants, and their names are straight out of the Good South Hall of Fame—heroes of the Movement, the Remnant, the Loyal Opposition, the moderate-progressive-liberal-black-white minority: John Lewis and Charles Morgan veteran civil rights activists; Reubin Askew, Julian Bond, Howard Lee and William Winter, practicing politicians; LeRoy Collins and Frank Smith, former practicing politicians; journalists Hodding Carter III, Eugene Patterson, Reese Cleghorn, and Pat Watters; educators Benjamin Mays and Joel Fleish-

I

man; John Hope Franklin, C. Vann Woodward and half a dozen other noted historians; foundation executives Harold Fleming and Leslie Dunbar, both former directors of the Southern Regional Council, an old and respected fraternity of the faithful.

On the last page of the program, after Credits (Budget Rent-a-Car, Anheuser-Busch, etc.), is a note inviting interested persons to write to "J. Silver, SOC 103, University of South Florida, Tampa." J. Silver is another Hall-of-Famer: James W. Silver, professor of history, author of *Mississippi: The Closed Society*, a refugee at Notre Dame for a while after his forced departure from Ole Miss, now back in the South and in the good graces of his adopted state.

What is this Symposium on the Contemporary South? Is it another christening for another New South? Is it an Irish wake for the late, great civil rights movement? Is it a convocation of latter-day Agrarians? Progressives? Populists? Jeremiahs? Is it a death-of-the-South debate, an academic navel-gazing exercise like the theologians had when God allegedly passed on a few years ago? Is it a revival meeting celebrating the South's return to the Union?

"It's a party," the man says, swirling bourbon and ice cubes in a plastic throwaway glass. "Jim Silver did it—he got some money from Ford and Field and SRC and the university, and he called up all his old cronies and invited them to a party."

"Naw, there's more to it than that," another man demurs. "It's for the benefit and enlightenment of the university's history faculty and students. This is a department of has-beens, never-wases, and not-yets. Silver is trying to elevate it. It's a great thing for them, bringing together a bunch of distinguished people like this. Nobody but a man of Silver's stature could pull it off. If you're interested in the South, it's an important gathering. There's probably never been anything like it."

"Well, you can't fault the guest list," says a third man in the little clutch of drinkers, looking around the room and speaking in a loud voice against the din of animated conversations. "But there are a lot of others who should be here."

They take turns tossing out names of absentees—Harry Ashmore, Will Campbell, Vincent Harding, Fannie Lou Hamer, Andrew Young, Vivian Henderson, Bill Emerson, Herman Long, Lerone Bennett, Tom Wicker, Terry Sanford, Ralph David Abernathy, Vernon Jordan, Johnny Popham, Tom Pettigrew, Charles Evers, Willie Morris. "Nobody has mentioned all the Legal Defense Fund attorneys," one of the men says, "or any women, or any young people. In fact, most of the people we've named, and most of the people who are here, are old—at least they're not young. If this is a symposium on the contemporary South, where are the contemporary people—the militants, the radicals?"

"Like who?"

None of them can think of any.

The symposium sessions are held in a theater in the center of the University of South Florida campus. The first night, when Julian Bond introduces Benjamin Mays, president emeritus of Morehouse College and now chairman of the Atlanta School Board, the auditorium is nearly full. In his speech, Dr. Mays says the last two decades "brought more basic changes in the black man's political, social, and economic positions than any comparable period since 1865." He also says it is his considered judgment "that the vast majority of white Americans, North and South . . . are segregationists at heart. . . . It is not merely the fact that the Supreme Court is forcing them to desegregate, but it is the belief on the part of many whites, perhaps millions upon millions, that white people are mentally superior to black folks."

Later, in a conversation about the Atlanta schools, Dr. Mays asserts that they may become like Washington's schools: all black. It is whites who control, he says, and it is they who will determine what Atlanta's schools become. "They say to me, 'What can we do?' And I say, 'Whatever you want, you'll get it. You always have. You'll make it happen.'"

Headquarters for the guests is at the Clearwater Beach Hilton, 38 miles from the campus. High-rise mock opulence on the Gulf of Mexico, an air-conditioned cocoon lined with vinyl wallpaper and nylon carpets, sheltering snowbirds from the hot and humid midday weather.

"Why the hell are we staying way out here?" a symposiast asks. "We'll spend half our time commuting."

"Jim wanted everybody to be able to enjoy the beach," comes the reply. "Some of the wives may not want to attend every session, and it's a lot more pleasant to be here on the water than over in Tampa."

The drive takes just over an hour. Part of it is on a causeway crossing Tampa Bay, a pleasant drive except at the rush hour. The rest is either on the interstate highway that cuts a wide, weaving swath through Tampa or, on the Clearwater side, a six-lane, stop-and-go excursion through Strip City—used-car lots, root beer stands, taco take-outs, a neon jungle. It could be anywhere in America.

At a morning panel discussion, Pat Watters and Hodding Carter are pessimistic about the approach of another New South. It could become a façade, they say, another betrayal of blacks, as happened after Reconstruction. Chuck Morgan, an American Civil Liberties Union attorney, agrees with them, but he comes out hopeful: "If there's any hope in this country, it's in the South. You can call that provincial, but that's the way it is."

They are followed by John Hope Franklin, the University of Chicago historian, whose address is about men who have recorded Southern history. The earliest of them, he says, "assumed that slavery was a positive good . . . that Reconstruction was an unmitigated evil," and they helped to persuade many non-Southerners that the white South's racial attitudes should be condoned if not imitated. Now, Dr. Franklin says, "many Southern historians, looking at the past of their own region and finding it wanting, have sought to make amends for that past by dealing honestly with the present."

At the end of Franklin's scholarly address, a white radical teacher in the audience, angered by the professor's dispassionate and nonmilitant approach, passes a written question to the podium: "Where did a nigger like you learn to talk so good?" The sort of question white supremacists used to shout has now been appropriated by their arch-enemies, the white revolutionaries.

Three of the leading contributors to the "new Southern history" praised by Dr. Franklin are next on the program: Dewey Grantham of Vanderbilt, Paul Gaston of Virginia, and George Tindall of North Carolina. Their message is that the often expressed hope that a late-developing South will profit from the mistakes of the North is probably a false hope. "If experience is any guide," says one of them, "we shall have to make the mistakes all over again. In fact, we started long ago. . . . The idea that change is a threat to be resisted is too deeply rooted in the Southern mind." And says another of them, the term "New South" is misleading anyway, and he adds: "Instead of a new Southern history, we need to tell the old one like it really was. It's a mistake to adopt a Yankee world view just when that view is crumbling."

Out on the causeway, the car radio carries an announcer's breathless message that the speaker for the annual Sales and Marketing Executives banquet will be Bart Starr, quarterback of the Green Bay Packers: "Bart Starr will be calling the signals, and *you* will be learning about *the* most important game: SUCCESS! Tickets are six dollars each, available at all your local banks."

The evening papers report that a federal judge in Richmond has ordered that city's mostly black school system merged with the predominantly white systems in two adjoining counties. And another story is datelined Baton Rouge:

"Two white deputy sheriffs and two Negro men were killed Monday in a battle of shotguns, pistols and tommyguns on a dingy street in Louisiana's capital city, during a demonstration by 1,000 blacks.

"Besides the four dead, at least 34 persons were injured, two critically, and 23 were arrested, after the melee in this town of 200,000."

Finally, on the editorial page, there is a report from the *Congressional Quarterly.* "President Nixon may or may not have a Southern strategy for being re-elected President," it says, "but he seems to have one for getting bills through Congress. In 1971, for the second year in a row, Southern senators and representatives supported Nixon more often than their colleagues from any other part of the country. The Southern support cut across party lines."

Eugene C. Patterson, former editor of the Atlanta *Constitution* and the Washington *Post* and now editor-designate of the St. Petersburg *Times,* is the next featured speaker on the schedule, his address to be delivered in a hotel in downtown St. Petersburg, another 25-mile drive south from Clearwater. The Tampa Bay area is a sort of Southern version of the San Francisco Bay megalopolis, and St. Petersburg is one of the points in the triangle. It is best known as a haven for retired white folks from all over, a sort of anteroom for the elderly, but its newspaper is young-looking and vigorous, one of the best.

Patricia Derian, national Democratic committeewoman from Mississippi, introduces Patterson. She is an attractive white woman who is simultaneously outspoken and soft-spoken. "You have not seen anyone else like me on the program thus far," she says. "I am what is known as a woman." The audience laughs nervously. "We have a New South for the middle classes, both white and black," she says, "but the gains in economics and civil rights in recent years have done little for the poor of either race—and that's nothing to be congratulatory about. I'm glad this meeting hasn't turned into a celebration of the New South." The first New South was coopted by Northern industrialists, she says, and this one may be dominated by the foundations: "If anything happens to the Ford Foundation, it'll be the end of the South." More nervous laughter.

Patterson, as if on cue, proceeds to celebrate the New South. He had announced the dawning of a new day in Southern politics thirty years ago, he says, when Ellis Arnall was elected governor of Georgia, and again in 1960, 1961, 1962, and 1964—and it was after all that that Lester Maddox took over. Nevertheless, he says, "believe it or not, I am going to tell you, quite seriously, that I do believe the South is on its way now— on its way out of the material and spiritual hard times it has known. . . . I have to believe that a newer politics is germinating in the Southern soil now; that the sprouting of the current crop of modern governors in many states is not just one more mutation in a region somehow fated to political famine."

Patterson ticks off some of the signs: rising per capita income, population growth, industrialization, national leadership in school desegregation, increased expenditures for education. There are still many problems, he acknowledges, but he is buoyantly optimistic: "What a powerful chapter it would be in American life if the white Southern people led their politicians into a final surrender of the struggle against our better selves and, in a kind of counter-Appomattox, stood free at last of the racial ball and chain that has chain-ganged the South long enough." That powerful chapter, he seems to be saying, is about to be written.

Cocktail hour again, before a sumptuous feast at Tampa's premier Spanish restaurant, Columbia. Little clusters of guests discuss the proceedings.

"What do you make of it all?" asks one.

"It means ten more years of the same old thing," a young black man answers.

"All I hear Patterson saying," another declares, "is that blacks are coming into the fold, and whites are accepting them. And all of us, black and white, are catching up with the rest of the country. Patt Derian had it right—that's nothing to celebrate about."

"Yeah," says the first man, "the South is losing its identity and the blacks are losing theirs—the former by homogenization and the latter by so-called integration, as it is defined by whites."

In his remarks earlier, Benjamin Mays had said: "The sad thing about all this [national statistics on school desegregation] is the fact that nothing seems to count toward integration except that which moves from black to white." The change is always on white terms. What the federal government (and many Southerners) considers "the completion of desegregation" results in a diminution of black teachers and administrators, closing of black schools, white flight from black majorities. It threatens the demise of public black colleges, and produces only token desegregation of most white ones. In the legislatures of the eleven Southern states in 1972, there were forty-two blacks—and 1,771 whites. The New South governors, says Patt Derian, "have learned the lingo." Things have changed. And things haven't.

Irony and contradiction also suffuses the after-dinner conversations. The guests scatter, and late in the evening small groups of them congregate again back at the Hilton. In one room, a clutch of Old Guard liberals, veterans all, reenact a ritual that is as old as Southern liberalism itself. They have

retained, miraculously, a sense of humor, an ability to laugh at
the South and at themselves. They sing a few songs, recall
humorous incidents, drink to the memory of departed fellow
warriors such as Ralph McGill and Bill Baggs. For a while, the
Second Reconstruction of the South was high on the national
agenda, and white liberals, as the support forces for their black
allies, were movers and shakers. Now the conventional wisdom
nationally is that it's all over—the South is reconstructed.
High up in the Clearwater Hilton, they know better, but they
also know that the chances of their being able to move and
shake again are almost gone. We are, says one of them with wit
and insight, "a convocation of emeritus liberals." It is like a
farewell to arms. And maybe it has always been like that:
Southern white liberals, the best of them, have seen themselves
as an outcast minority with no real power and only limited
influence, and they have accepted that reality and gone on
trying anyway.

The next day's agenda features Reese Cleghorn of the
Charlotte *Observer;* William Winter, the newly elected lieutenant governor of Mississippi; Frank Smith, a former Mississippi congressman and a director of the Tennessee Valley
Authority; and John Lewis, leader in the registration of new
black voters in the South as director of the Voter Education
Project. "If there's not a New South, what is the lieutenant
governor of Mississippi doing at a meeting like this?" Winter
asks. His state, he says, is on the eve of a new era. Smith, too,
asserts that the South is surrendering at last its preoccupation
with race. Lewis, at thirty-two a battle-scarred veteran of the
struggle for black liberation, exhibits the quiet determination
that led him to sign on for the duration fifteen years ago: "It is
important to remember that our struggle is not for a month, a
season, a year, but for a lifetime, if that is what it takes to
build the Beloved Community." And Cleghorn is still looking
for substance behind the New South rhetoric. What we've had

is a change in style, he says, but all the old problems remain, and no really new political mechanism has been fashioned to cope with them. From the new governors we hear the good words and the music, but where is the action, where are the programs?

One of the governors, Florida's Reubin Askew, is scheduled for an evening address. Five minutes before he comes from backstage to the podium, about thirty black students file silently down the aisles flanking the auditorium. They hold hand-lettered signs: BLACK FOLKS HAVE NEVER KNOWN ANY NEW SOUTHERN POLITICS. SOUTHERN HISTORY EQUALS NEW SLAVERY, JIVE RECONSTRUCTION, UNENFORCED CIVIL RIGHTS, CHEAP WELFARE, WHITE SYMPOSIUM. They march quietly into the orchestra pit in front of the podium and take seats just as Askew appears. He gets a standing ovation from the rest of the audience, but the black protesters remain seated, holding their signs aloft.

If there is a genuine article in the showcase of New South governors, Askew may well be it. In an act of rare political courage—some call it suicide—he has told the people of his state that segregation and inequality of opportunity, not busing, should be the target of all who want quality in the schools, and he has said that if busing is necessary to put an end to segregation, he is for it. Handsome and youthful-looking, he exudes sincerity. He talks about "the maturing South . . . a humanistic South, which has always been there, just below the surface of racism and despair, struggling for a chance to emerge," and he says that chance may have arrived at last: "I believe the people of the South aren't going to merely join the Union. They're going to be faced with the opportunity, perhaps even the responsibility, to lead it." Askew says the time for change has never been so ripe: "The South tomorrow can represent the coming of age of an entire people—culturally, economically, educationally, socially, politically. It won't be easy. We have a very long way to go." But, he asserts, we are on the way, headed in the right direction at last.

It goes down well with the audience. Even the skeptics like it, and him. He gets another standing ovation, and then leaves for a reception in his honor in a nearby building on the campus. The audience is invited, and when the scene has shifted the black students are there too, their protest signs stashed away. They are in the reception line, exchanging soul shakes with the governor (he does it expertly), laughing and talking with him. There is not even a nervous look among the plain-clothes policemen in the room—all of them are relaxed and smiling. It all could not have gone more smoothly if it had been rehearsed.

While Askew has been in Tampa winning new supporters with his sincerity, another Southern governor is in Tallahassee announcing his candidacy for the Democratic presidential nomination. George Wallace is also for real: the Florida primary is two months away, and he is already favored to win it. The contrast between Askew and Wallace, and the popular appeal of both men in Florida, defies explanation; they are Southerners, speaking from and for the South, speaking to the nation, yet saying very different things.

And the South they speak from is doing very different things. A reading of the region's newspapers underscores the ambiguity:

• A federal court in Montgomery has ordered reapportionment of the Alabama legislature into single-member districts of equal size. Estimates based on black voter registration indicate that about thirty blacks would probably be elected under such a plan. There are two blacks in the Alabama House and Senate now, and 138 whites.

• A survey of prisons in six Southern states shows that seven of every ten inmates on death row are black.

• A story from Atlanta says moderate black organizations

such as the NAACP and the Southern Christian Leadership Conference are "slipping from their positions at the top of Atlanta's black power pyramid," and the Black Panthers and Black Muslims are gaining followers.

• In Marianna, Arkansas, black students were fire-hosed and arrested in a protest demonstration at a local desegregated high school.

• Two reporters for the Charlotte *Observer,* analyzing some unpublished census figures, report that while Florida gained 1.3 million people through in-migration during the 1960s, the other ten Southern states lost 660,000 residents to states outside the South. Black out-migration, which many people have been saying is all over, was heavier than expected: almost 1.5 million blacks left the South for other points during the decade.

• In Warren County, North Carolina, one-time black firebrand Floyd McKissick, former director of CORE, is building Soul City, a new town, with the support and encouragement of the Nixon administration.

• At least two blacks—Andrew Young in Atlanta and Barbara Jordan in Houston—are favored to win seats in the U.S. House of Representatives next fall, and blacks will be running in several other districts in the South.

Gone are the days of one-crop agriculture, one-party politics, one-faith religion, one-race supremacy. And nowhere is there a clear vision of what will replace them.

The last session of the symposium belongs to former Florida governor LeRoy Collins, to Joel Fleishman of Duke University, to another North Carolinian—black mayor Howard Lee of Chapel Hill—and to historian C. Vann Woodward of Yale, who is probably the nation's foremost Southern scholar. Collins asks to be counted "on the optimistic side" in the appraisal of the South's future, though he acknowledges that white attitudes of racial superiority remain widespread. Fleishman, a key figure in Terry Sanford's administration at Duke University, asserts that the South is already changing very rapidly, and the challenge is to stop talking about the New South and start taking steps to keep it from becoming like the North. Lee, who is also a candidate for Congress, says he believes in the dream of a New South, but he asks where we are now, and he answers his own question by citing a record that contains as much shadow as substance and leaves the dream deferred.

The last word about the contemporary South is left to Professor Woodward. Those who in the past indulged in predictions about the South's future tended to be pessimists, he says—and things have usually turned out even worse than they expected. As for the optimists, of course, they were even further from the mark. He recalls that it was Henry Grady, the famous editor of the Atlanta *Constitution,* who launched the first New South movement almost a hundred years ago—a movement which ended in "separate but equal" segregation. Grady's New South was the spitting image of Yankeedom, Woodward says, and he adds: "We are, in fact, still living with the progressive realization of Grady's dream of a Yankeefied South. Every new throughway, every new supermarket, every central city is an extension of it. The full horror of it is suggested only slightly by a drive between Tampa and Clearwater. I wonder if what the South really wants is uncritical emulation of the North."

He praises Askew's speech for its vision of the South as leader and pacesetter, and he allows himself to wonder if "we may be witnessing something new and hopeful in the South." The distance between Askew and his predecessor, Claude Kirk, "must be measured in light years. It almost tempts a hardened skeptic to believe in progress. Almost."

And there it ends—five days of talking and listening, 500 miles of commuting, an intellectual tug-of-war between optimism and pessimism. There are no clear winners, no safe conclusions to draw.

At the Fisherman's Wharf, across the street from the Clearwater Hilton, some of the guests share one more round of food and drink before going their separate ways. It has been a movable feast, both literally and figuratively. Jim Silver is there at the end, picking up the tab. He has taken no part in the formal program, has made no pronouncements about the South to be recorded for the ages with those of his friends, and in that he may prove to be the wisest of them all.

"There's a symposium on the 'Mind of the South' coming up in Chapel Hill in March," somebody says, "and they say it's going to be the New South conference to end all New South conferences." Silver's ruddy, wrinkled face forms a little smile. He looks out toward the beach, where a few gulls and a pelican are gliding lazily in the shimmering heat.

"The idea was to have a good time," he says to no one in particular. "But the other—the conference itself—turned out pretty well too."

Nobody convenes New North conferences, or symposiums on the Contemporary Midwest, or seminars on the Mind of the East; it is only Southerners who seem to have something elusive and indefinable in the psyche that compels them to think of themselves as different from other Americans. For longer than there has been a United States of America there has been a South, and for almost that long, Southerners have been congregating to talk about themselves and their region, gathering in groups defined by religion or race or class or family or political ideology, and investing those gatherings with a regional self-consciousness that has often transcended and overshadowed all else.

After Tampa in 1972 there was Chapel Hill, where a group of University of North Carolina students planned and staged a two-week exploration of "The Mind of the South—The Southern Soul." Then, in Birmingham, there was a meeting of the L. Q. C. Lamar Society, which identifies itself as "a non-profit, tax-exempt educational organization committed to the premise that Southerners can find practical solutions to the South's major problems." Later in the year, there was the annual meeting in Atlanta of the Southern Regional Council, a biracial body that has worked for more than thirty years to improve race relations and social conditions in the South. And finally, in December, there was a two-day civil rights symposium at the University of Texas in Austin, where former President Lyndon B. Johnson made the last speech of his long political career— and ended it, ironically, with words he had borrowed once before to signify his commitment to civil rights: "We shall overcome."

With the exception of the Austin meeting, which was more of a national than a regional affair, the South itself was the subject of all those convocations, and even in Austin there was an unmistakable Southern accent: Lyndon Johnson was a Southerner, and during his administration civil rights was a Southern preoccupation. The 1972 conferences also presupposed a belief in racial equality, and while that is by no means a part of every convocation of Southerners (the Ku Klux Klan still exists, and so does the Citizens Council), there aren't many meetings any more to "preserve the Southern way of life," because the "Southern way of life" to most people meant unrestrained white supremacy enforced by law, and that is all over.

So it is mostly Southerners with a particular perspective— for want of a better term, it is Southern liberals—who still gather to talk introspectively about their region, and where it has been, and where it is going. It is, paradoxically, liberal blacks and whites who now seek to preserve their own vision of the South—or to create a vision—and save it from inundation beneath the homogenizing tide of American nationalism.

The white supremacists, in their heyday, had their own version of "the Southern way of life." So did the Agrarians, a group of Southern intellectuals who, more than forty years ago, attempted to define "a Southern way of life against what

may be called the American or prevailing way." Their aim was
to stop the headlong advance of industrial and urban growth.
Around the turn of the last century, the Populists in the South
came close to forging a union of black and white working-class
people. In the final decades of the nineteenth century, the New
South movement identified with Henry Grady tried to initiate a
Southern renaissance based on economic growth. Reconstruction was another period when people tried to define a different
social order—the very name suggests what was envisioned—
and the Civil War itself was the most extreme instance of
change in the South. Before the war, pro-slavery advocates and
abolitionists rallied to their respective causes with the fiercest
sort of dedication. All of those groups—the slavery advocates,
the abolitionists, the Reconstructionists, the New South evangelists, the Populists, the Agrarians, the latter-day white supremacists, the civil rights movement forces, and now the
remnant of liberal integrationists—have had one thing in
common: they have looked upon the South as being funda-
mentally different from the rest of the country. Some have
tried to retain and perpetuate the difference they saw; some
have tried to eradicate the difference; some have tried to create
a wholly new but still distinctive entity. As long as there are
people who think of the South as another place, another
region, a separate entity, there will no doubt be movements to
change it, wars to preserve it, plans to transform it or adopt it
or exploit it.

So the Southerners who gathered in 1972 in Tampa and
Chapel Hill and Birmingham and Atlanta were following in a
long regional tradition. Like all of the gatherings and movements and convocations before theirs, going back well over a
century, the 1972 meetings grew out of an acute regional consciousness, a view of the South as a separate place. In the
perspective of history, they probably should not be considered
important meetings. In no sense were they pivotal; they did
not perpetuate anything, or change anything, or create any-

thing. But as an aid to understanding the contemporary South, they are a valuable resource.

In the ten years prior to 1972, the South witnessed the decline and fall of legalized white supremacy, the waxing and waning of the civil rights movement, and the appearance of another New South ideology. Black Americans, with the aid of the courts and some white liberal allies, rose up against intolerable conditions of discrimination and poverty, and in a classic confrontation with the perpetrators of white supremacy, the blacks achieved a historic Southern victory. The fight for equality and justice then spread northward, into the cities and the universities, and the focus shifted from civil rights to the war in Vietnam and to broader inequities in the American political and social structure. While conditions for blacks and poor people in the South were somewhat improved, racism was being rediscovered in the North, and poverty was suddenly visible again among all races in all parts of the country. Urban riots and assassinations and military atrocities haunted the American conscience. Because the South seemed relatively better off than it had been, and because so much was wrong elsewhere, the South was finished as a national issue, and the people who remained there were left to work out their own accommodations to one another outside the glare of the national spotlight.

White supremacy was down, but not out. The civil rights movement had won some battles, but not the war. The South was changed, and still changing; it was becoming less and less distinct from the other regions of the country. After being set apart by compulsion and by choice for many decades, it was finally rejoining the Union. Almost no one any longer denied or defended what the South once was, and almost everyone acknowledged that it was not what it used to be. And the nation, too, was changing; in the evolution of its collective political thought and its racial attitudes, it was moving closer to the South. George Wallace's popularity in the North and

Richard Nixon's in the South are illustrative of the point, and so is the nationwide furor over school busing, and the phenomenon of white flight.

Under those conditions, the reemergence of a New South movement was probably inevitable. Moderate governors were in office in most of the Southern states, and they were talking confidently of a new day for blacks and whites alike; blacks were visible and influential in politics and business and education and religion, in virtually every aspect of life; the economy of every Southern state seemed healthy, and most were stronger than they had ever been. It was certainly time, past time, for a new South.

But serious problems still remained. The Nixon administration seemed intent on halting the advance of civil rights and civil liberties, and it was pressuring the courts to do likewise. Racial issues were far more complex than before; they no longer centered on dual school systems and segregated restaurants and denial of voting rights, but on standardized test scores and heredity-environment debates and school busing and seniority systems and quotas and black nationalism and community control and economic power and dozens more, all sophisticated and complicated. The South's cities were growing, and industrial development was advancing rapidly, and that meant jobs and money, but it also meant grief: growth and expansion brought exploitation of natural resources, disfiguration of the landscape, displacement of people, pollution of the air and the water. It brought urban decay and suburban sprawl, automation and depersonalization, conformity and monotony. In the political arena, one-party rule was just about over, but that had not turned out to be the panacea many people thought it would be. And in everyday life, the gap between rich and poor seemed as wide as ever, and as impossible to close.

In the Americanization of Dixie—and in the Southernization of America—the South and the nation seemed in many ways to be imitating the worst in each other, exporting vices without importing virtues; there was no spiritual or cultural or social balance of payments. The South was becoming more urban, less overtly racist, less self-conscious and defensive, more affluent—and more uncritically accepting of the ways of the North. And the North, for its part, seemed more overtly racist than it had been; shorn of its pretensions of moral innocence, it was exhibiting many of the attitudes that once were thought to be the exclusive possession of white Southerners.

In his book *Farewell to the South*, Robert Coles records these words of a Southerner in the Ku Klux Klan: "I think the South is going to be rescued by the North. I never would have dreamed that we have so many friends up there, but we do. It's in the white man's blood to stay clear of the nigger. . . . The South isn't being looked down on anymore. Today everyone's from the South, you could say; that's because everything we've been fighting for all along, the plain white people from down here, is what . . . people like us in other sections of the country are fighting for." That remark was made in 1968, when the antibusing controversy was building. But two years later, the same man said to Coles: "But what's the use? You can't fight and beat the inevitable. And I'll tell you this: I believe it's inevitable that the South is going to die. That's right: The South isn't going to be anymore. We're going the way of the rest of the country."

The Klansman's hope is the Southern liberal's despair: that the South is going to be rescued by the North, that Northern white racism, with all its sophistication and finesse, will save Southern white supremacy from extinction. But the Klansman's despair—that the South is going the way of the rest of the country—is a despair the liberal can understand and even share, however different his reasons for doing so.

The Southerners who came together in Tampa in 1972 to contemplate the past and the future of their region were understandably ambivalent about such things as the pace and style of desegregation, the rebirth of a New South creed, and the Americanization of the South. They expressed, for the most part, a collective mood of skepticism and pessimism: legal segregation was gone, but segregation still existed in fact; desegregation had not become integration, and integration— true equity—had hardly been tried at all; urbanization and industrialization were proving to be mixed blessings; the South was blindly repeating the old mistakes of the North; economic power was still controlled almost exclusively by whites; things were different but not always better, changing but also more complex, moving swiftly but not necessarily going anywhere. What was the South becoming? Was it enough simply to join the Union, to fall in at the rear of the ranks? Had the South learned anything from its past? Did it have anything to contribute to the nation's future? Was the South's admission fee to the Union going to be a surrender of assets and a nationalization of liabilities?

The pessimism of the Tampa conferees does not seem misplaced. The South is now closer to being like the rest of America than it has ever been. Its racial and economic and urban and political characteristics are very nearly the same as the dominant characteristics of the nation. The mobility of people and the diffusion of cultures through television and other media have advanced the process of Americanization to a new level. The lesson of the historians is that the South has never made a practice of learning from the mistakes of others, or from its own; if it remains true to form, it will keep on going through the open door into the Union, emulating unquestioningly the values and venalities of the big house.

If there was a consensus among the speakers in Tampa, it was not that the South's entry to the Union is a bad thing, but rather that Union alone is not enough; the more critical issue is the character of the new body. They seemed to be saying this: Integration of regions into a nation—like the integration of races and classes into a people—can be a great achievement. But it must be based on equity, and not on any notions of inferiority or superiority; it must be respectful and apprecia- tive of differences, not destructive of them. The success or failure of any attempt at unity depends upon what each party gains and loses, what each gives and receives, what each sur- renders and retains. Integration should mean neither domina- tion nor conformity—in this instance, neither the domination of the North over the South nor the creation of a bland and monotonously undifferentiated Union.

By those standards, the Americanization of Dixie as it is now proceeding falls far short of its promise. There is no parity, no equity. It is like the nation's approach to racial integration: the terms are set by the majority, and the burden of sacrifice and change and responsibility falls mostly on the minority. There has been enough change to break the logjam and loose the mighty American mainstream over the South, but it is not enough to make equality a reality. Whatever label it is given—the New South, the New America—it is too much like the New Chevy, or the New Wheaties, or the New Nixon: the same goods in a different package.

The words of Benjamin Mays in Tampa come readily to mind, and they bear repeating. He said three things: First, blacks have made more political and social and economic gains in the past two decades than in any comparable period since the Civil War. Second, it is whites who control: "They say to me, 'What can we do?' And I say, 'Whatever you want, you'll get it. You always have. You'll make it happen.'" And third, his personal view "that the vast majority of white Americans, North and South . . . are segregationists at heart. . . . It is not merely the fact that the Supreme Court is forcing them to desegregate, but it is the belief on the part of many whites, perhaps millions upon millions, that white people are mentally superior to black folks."

The people who met in Tampa—and many other Southerners as well, in all racial groups and economic classes and political parties—no doubt believe the South has had, and still has, some unique qualities. As a Southerner, I have so believed, and do believe. No long enumeration is necessary— there are books enough about the moonlight and magnolias, the courtesy and kinship, the friendliness and hospitality, the importance of things personal and concrete, the sense of pace and place and space and grace and soul. But beneath all that, the single most enduring and notorious characteristic of the South has been white racism. Journalist and nonpareil Southerner Joseph B. Cumming, Jr., has called it "a sort of state religion . . . a *sacred*, not a *secular*, 'way of life.' " Another native Southerner, *Ebony* magazine's Lerone Bennett, has described it as "the cornerstone of the Southern mystique." The worst manifestations of that racism are disappearing. Gone are the days of rampant, unbridled white supremacy up and down the Southern landscape, and gone are the blatant acts of cruelty and depravity—slavery, lynching, castration— and gone are most if not all of the preachers and teachers and historians and lawyers and politicians who gave their blessing to such acts. But what remains is a style and pace and form of white advantage—a more sophisticated racism—that differs little from South to North to West. The one thing that above all else made the South different—the way its white majority treated its black minority—is no longer very different from the way it is done in the rest of America. And the softening of the white South's racial attitudes—or more accurately, their diffusion nationwide—seems sufficient to remove the last barrier to the Americanization of Dixie. The qualities worth keeping— the grace and pace and soul and all the rest—seem less likely to survive.

Regional and personal identity have always been important to Southerners. It has mattered greatly whether you were for segregation or against it, whether you were its beneficiary or its victim. It has mattered whether you were white, or black, or a woman, or a Baptist, or a Democrat, or Mr. Bob So-and-So's boy. It has mattered that you were a Southerner, whether black or white, male or female, young or old, rich or poor. Because the South was different, every person who lived there was defined, identified, by that difference. It was because of race that those things mattered, no doubt, but under more equitable circumstances, such personal identity in an impersonal world would surely be an asset. But with the coming of a new identity—a national identity—regional and personal consciousness seems already to be diminishing. There are more and more people living in the South who do not think of themselves as Southerners, and consequently there are fewer and fewer who think of the South as a separate region, and believe it deeply enough to fight for its preservation or its reconstruction or its destruction. Perhaps that is why only a few liberals and intellectuals and integrationists and grass-roots folks still gather to talk self-consciously about their lives and their land, and to warn against repeating the North's mistakes, and to dream of a national renaissance of civility being generated in the South, and to worry about President Nixon's Southern strategy of 1968–72 destroying the second Reconstruction, as President Rutherford B. Hayes destroyed the first one with the Compromise of 1877.

After the Tampa and Chapel Hill gatherings, Joe Cumming wrote about them in an article for *Georgia* magazine. "The South seems to have an incurable impulse for bittersweet goodbys to itself," he said. "It is a posturing usually followed by a few boasting, boosterish 'hi there's' to some brand-name New South. . . . Twice already this year I have attended symposiums in the South, on the South, that resonated with 'this is the last' and 'this is the first.' Now I come to tell you this: it is over this time. Finished and done. The Old South *and* the New South. That is to say, the South as a separate, self-conscious concept is simply no longer fascinating. . . . The curtain has come down; the world has gone home."

There, in essence, is what the Americanization of Dixie is all about. The South as a land of grace and violence, as beauty and the beast, had an irresistible fascination about it. It was evil and decadent, but it also bred heroes and dreamers, and it yielded a tenacious sense of hopefulness that kept the world from going home. It still has qualities that could make the world come back for another look. But it is well on the way to a surrender of its distinctiveness, to amalgamation in the nation, at a time when the nation is still groping, after two hundred years, for a society in harmony with the principles on which it was founded.

The United States has always been a diverse nation, diverse in its geography, its resources, its culture, its institutions, its people. Diversity is probably its most valuable and abundant possession—and its most unappreciated resource. America has also been a nation pledged to the pursuit of lofty ideals—liberty, justice, equality. But its people have tended to perceive of diversity and equality as being mutually exclusive. We have promoted advantage based on race and income and social class. Being different has meant being better or worse, and the melting-pot theory has served that notion: Be like us, like the majority, or be excluded.

Now the ideal of equality is threatened, and the fact of diversity is under assault; without attaining the former, the nation seems intent on destroying the latter. Instead of equality and diversity, the choices are the melting pot and apartheid.

It would be the crowning irony if the South should somehow contribute vital leadership in a reconstruction of the American spirit. It knows from its own experience something about defeat and reconstruction, and it knows, too, that apartheid will not work. Perhaps it could teach as well as learn, lead as well as follow. But so far, there is not much in the record to encourage hope that creative approaches to an American renaissance will emanate from the South. Here and there, singular people and places and events break the pattern, but the dominant trends are clear: Northern-style urbanization and industrialization, continuing segregation and discrimination in education and housing and economics, homogenization of tastes and cultures, unrelenting poverty and malnutrition, a national Southern strategy dominating politics and government, exploitation of the land and the natural resources.

The modern, acquisitive, urban, industrial, post-segregationist, on-the-make South, its vices nationalized, its virtues evaporating if not already dissipated, is coming back to the Mother Country, coming back with a bounce in its step, like a new salesman on the route, eager to please, intent on making it.

There ain't no revolution.

Agriculture: Harvest Time for the Family Farm

Herschel Ligon had left the hayfield at eight o'clock, in the last hour of daylight. At half past nine, still in his work clothes, he was sitting on a straight-back chair in his living room, talking about his favorite subject, the consuming interest in his life—farming. His supper was still waiting in the kitchen, but he seemed in no hurry for it.

"My farm, and my sister's farm next to me, and my daddy's farm across the road, has never belonged to anybody but the family," he said. "It was granted to my great-great-grandfather for his service in the Revolutionary War. We've got about three hundred acres altogether. I'm the fifth generation to farm here. The house my father and mother live in is the oldest house in this county, built in 1791. I was born in that house fifty-five years ago."

He paused to reflect a moment, and when he spoke again his

words were deliberate and direct: "I don't mind telling you this: One of the reasons I'm so active in trying to solve this farm problem is, I hate to be the last farmer of this family. But unless the economic situation changes, I will be, because I can't conscientiously encourage my boys to farm when they can't make a living at it."

Herschel Ligon represents a body of Americans which once outnumbered all others combined, but which now makes up less than 5 percent of the total population: he is a family farmer, a free-enterprise farmer. If he does not become the last of his lineage to work the land his ancestors settled, it will be because he is willing to work twelve- and fifteen-hour days, including weekends, winter and summer, or because he is willing to incur large debts, or because he feels honor-bound by 180 years of family history, or because he loves farming enough to keep at it, or because he sees no acceptable alternative. Or because, to use his words, "I'm just too damn stubborn to quit."

As an individual human being, Ligon is not easily forgotten. He is courteous and polite, almost courtly, and he is also informed and articulate. Farming is not only what he does with skill and efficiency; it is also what he *knows*, what he understands. He can place what he has experienced on his farm in the context of what he has observed about agriculture in the United States, and his interpretation of those experiences and observations is impressive and compelling.

But as a statistic, he is a diminishing figure, a fading image. In 1940, more than 30 million people lived on farms in this country. There were 6,350,000 farms then, with an aggregate of more than one billion acres, and the average farm had about 160 acres. In round figures now, the farm population has declined to 9 million, the number of farms has diminished to 2,800,000, total farm acreage has *increased* by 60 million acres, and the average farm has 400 acres. What those figures show is the coming extinction of the small farmer and the corresponding rise of the corporate giant.

Agribusiness conglomerates have become the controlling forces in American agriculture, and their power is attested to by everything from government policies to trends in research and technology. One of the consequences of mass-production agriculture, intentional or not, is the exploitation (and often the elimination) of the unlanded rural poor—sharecroppers, tenant farmers, migrant laborers. The landed rural poor—Southerners, for the most part, people with less than 50 acres of land and only the most rudimentary implements to work it with—don't fare much better in competition with modern practitioners. Survival is a more realistic goal for them than prosperity is, and the recent growth of agricultural coopera-tives among the poor at least offers some hope that they will be able to stay on the land without starving.

Between the desperately poor and the impersonal giants of agriculture is the Middle American family farmer. He has accumulated some acreage and perhaps a little rainy-day money, he has carried on a family farm tradition, he has made at least a modest success out of his life's work. He is white, black, brown, a Southerner, Northerner, Westerner. If you want to know what is happening to American agriculture now, and what is going to happen, the middle-class farmer is the man to watch. In the evolving American way of life, he is a threatened species.

Herschel Ligon is one of them, one of the vanishing breed, and he is all the more conspicuous because he refuses to quit. The invisible ones have already given up; they appear now in the statistics as factory workers and urban dwellers. Ligon stands out because he speaks out; he is a Jeremiah in brogans and khaki pants, a warning voice in the emptying rural countryside.

The land Ligon farms with his eighty-five-year-old father is on U.S. Highway 70 between Nashville and Lebanon, Tennessee. President Andrew Jackson's famous country home, the Hermitage, is three miles down the highway, and Old Hickory Lake, a Corps of Engineers impoundment, can be glimpsed in the distance from Ligon's backyard. Closer to the house, pleated hills roll and weave in soft curves of green, and sheep and cattle graze there in a scene of pastoral peacefulness. But impinging suburbia is also visible: a mobile home subdivision sits just to the east of the pasture, and boxy new brick homes pop up in spreading clusters, and a shopping center has opened nearby.

Ligon is a livestock farmer, raising about 200 head of hogs, cattle, and sheep at a time, and growing about 100 acres of grain and hay to provide roughly half the feed his animals require. Except when his youngest son is home from college, the only help he has is what his elderly father is able to provide; his oldest son has already graduated from college, and now is in charge of the University of Tennessee's hog and sheep herds.

About ten years ago, with his own economic situation worsening steadiy and with agriculture in a state of approaching chaos nationwide, Ligon began to think in terms of radical solutions. He came up with a disarmingly simple idea, and it has obsessed him ever since. Reduced to its barest essentials, the idea is this: Anybody who earns at least two-thirds of his annual income from the sale of agriculture products produced by him on the farm should be designated as a "Registered Farmer"; the federal government should guarantee 100 percent parity of price for all such agriculture products sold by Registered Farmers.

He is now the unpaid president of Registered Farmers of America, Inc. To the extent that the demands of his farm permit, he goes looking for allies, making speeches to political groups and labor union leaders and college students and civic clubs. He has testified before agriculture committees in both houses of Congress, and in 1968 he helped draft an agriculture plank for George Wallace's platform when the Alabama governor ran for president. To one and all, he says the same thing: Make farming profitable for people who live on farms and earn their livelihood from them. Take all controls off agriculture products, and let competition in the marketplace determine the price. Let people be able to buy cheap food. Let the government pay farmers the difference between the established true value of a product and the price it brings on the open market.

"Our program is simply this," Ligon said, sitting in his living room. "We want everybody who wants to farm to be able to make a decent living for his family and himself—that's all." Nothing radical about that—or is there? It would mean that Senator James Eastland could no longer draw $147,000 a year not to plant cotton on his Mississippi plantation. It would mean that American and foreign conglomerates with vast landholdings and only an incidental interest in farming could no longer be subsidized by the federal government for holding land out of production. It would mean that the government would not be paying out more than $3 billion a year to nonproducing nonfarmers. And it would mean that many of the more than 100,000 employees of the U.S. Department of Agriculture, one of the largest branches of the federal bureaucracy, would no longer be needed.

Ligon's vision does not stop there. "If you make farming profitable for real farmers," he says, "people who love the land will return to it. They could pay their debts, and pay their taxes. People who have migrated to the cities because they couldn't make a decent living on the farm would come back. We could balance the economy, and make the price of food reasonable, and give a lot of people a new sense of purpose. We have withered the wealth of the world—that's agriculture. A dollar spent by a farmer puts seven dollars into the nation's economy. If we eliminate the unfair competition of nonfarmers and guarantee Registered Farmers one hundred percent parity of price, in five years we can turn this nation's economy around and bring prosperity back for everybody."

Agriculture economists and U.S. Department of Agriculture people tell Ligon his plan is unrealistic. They say the advance of technology has rendered ideas like his obsolete. "My counterargument to them is that technology costs money," he says. "Hell, we're not as well off now producing a hundred and fifty bushels of corn as we used to be producing fifty bushels. It used to be that if you had a mule or horse, a plow, a double shovel, a harrow and a wagon, you could have a crop of corn. You didn't pay sixteen dollars a bushel for seed corn then— you went in the crib and shelled it. Today you've got to plant hybrid seed, and spray it; you can't gather it by hand; you've got to fertilize it, and because high fertilization doesn't produce corn that will dry naturally, you have to buy a dryer. You have to have a tractor, and a picker-sheller. So when you get through, you haven't got as much money as you had when you were doing it the other way. The technology they're talking about is on a note down at the bank."

Herschel Ligon talks about his scheme with sincerity and conviction and excitement. He has all the zeal and persuasiveness of an evangelist, a true believer. Yet for all his enthusiasm, there is in his voice and in his expression—and in unguarded moments, in his words—a hint of his other self: Ligon the realist, the pragmatist, the man who understands human nature and the fickleness of fate. He has congressmen tell him privately that his plan eventually has to come about, that it's nothing in the world but good common sense, but they are silent when public debate begins. He knows the power of big business, and he knows that nobody has ever been able to organize the nation's farmers, and he knows that the advance of technology is probably inevitable. He knows he is one man against many:

"I guess I wouldn't say I'm hopeful about our chances—just stubborn, maybe. I think it can be done, but it's gonna be tough. If I had the time to speak night and day, and the money to put on an advertising campaign. . . ." He has been the route of existing agricultural organizations—the Farm Bureau, the National Farmers Organization, the Grange—and each time he has come away frustrated. Registered Farmers is his alternative effort. It has a small number of members in Tennessee, Alabama, and Kentucky. He is fighting for survival—his, and family agriculture's. And he is losing.

"I tell you what's gonna happen," he says. "When they liquidate people like me, big business is gonna take over agriculture production—and do you think big business is stupid enough to sell their production for the prices I've been getting for the past twenty years? Hell, no. And don't you know they're good enough organizers to get together—there's not gonna be but a few of them, anyway—and raise the prices. They can't produce as efficiently as I can. They're gonna have to pay union labor—time and a half for overtime. One day last winter I brought a calf in out of the snow, saved two sets of twin lambs, and farrowed three sows, all in twenty-four hours. I never took my clothes off—and it was a Sunday to boot. Where you gonna get the labor to do that? Where you gonna get people as wrapped up in the thing, as in love with the job as that? So big business will make the consumer pay, and the American people could be spending half their income on food, like they are in Russia."

In 1972, six bags of protein feed for his hogs cost Ligon between $30 and $35. A year later, the same feed cost him $104. Corn that was $1.35 a bushel had gone up to $2.85. The prospect of a property tax increase loomed, and soaring land values seemed certain to mean higher taxes for him. Dogs from the nearby subdivisions had been killing his sheep. Even the weather seemed to carry a message: rain all but ruined his hay. "I'm no saint, but I do believe in divine guidance," he said, smiling faintly. "And I just wonder if the Lord has decided that since we've misused this great nation of ours, this wealth and abundance, I just wonder if he's decided to cut the food off, to see if he can't straighten us out."

Ligon is brimming over with facts and figures; he's like a

walking almanac. "In 1965, of the hundred and nineteen millionaires farming, only sixteen paid income tax." "For the past twenty years, the producers of agriculture have been underpaid an average of forty and a half billion dollars a year." "Forty-one cents out of every dollar goes for taxes, twenty-six cents for interest, twenty cents for debt payment—that leaves the average man thirteen cents to buy the cheapest food in the world, and that food costs sixteen cents." He has other facts and figures too: his income, his fixed costs, his debts. They don't add up either. "Both my boys tell me they'd love to come back here and farm, and I'd love for them to. I hate to be the last. But I don't know. I just don't know."

Herschel Ligon is not in danger of losing his land because somebody rich and powerful covets it—not yet, anyway. His land is jeopardized because it is becoming more and more difficult for him to make a living on it. Unlike many farmers in locations where no growth and development is taking place, Ligon could at least expect to get a good price for his land if he decided to sell it, but that is no consolation for him—he wants to farm the land, not sell it. Yet he is enmeshed in a complex of economic problems that are not of his making, and he is virtually powerless to do anything about them.

In 1971 the National Broadcasting Company produced a television documentary on rural migration that vividly portrayed the consequences of forcing farmers off the land. It contrasted overcrowded cities with deserted farms, and it described the growth of agribusiness conglomerates, and the effects of government policies and technological research. These issues, said commentator Garrick Utley, "are not confined to any one area of the country. They cut across racial and regional lines. It is a national problem. A national crisis."

Herschel Ligon is living proof of Utley's observation. He is not facing economic disaster because he is a farmer in the South, but because he is a farmer, period. He has thousands of counterparts in the Midwest, the West, the North—wherever people farm. Nebraska lost 73,000 people in the 1960s, and 20,000 of its farms went out of business. The fading family farmer is a national phenomenon.

Still, the South *is* agriculture—or used to be—and Ligon's farm is not very representative of the agricultural South. It was never a plantation, it never produced a cotton crop, it never depended on black and poor white sharecroppers and tenant farmers, it isn't remote from the burgeoning cities. There were many such farms in the Deep South—and they, too, are fading.

Jim Williams used to be a cotton farmer in Crenshaw County, Alabama. He lived in a rambling white frame house about five miles out of Luverne, the county seat, and his land stretched about him farther than the eye could see—about 10,000 acres in all, give or take a couple thousand.

The heyday for Jim Williams was the late 1930s—after the Depression and before the war. He had four boys, all in or near their twenties, and a wife and three daughters, and he had about fifty tenant families, black and white, living in cabins dotted across the farm. There was a cotton gin, and a commissary, and a sawmill, and a warehouse, and with about 5,000 acres in cultivation, there was plenty of work to be done, and plenty of reward in it for the Williams family. They butchered hogs enough to fill the smokehouse with hams and sausage and slabs of bacon, and they canned fruits and vegetables and preserves to line the pantry shelves, and they killed chickens for Sunday dinner. They raised some peanuts, but cotton was the big cash crop, and in a good year the land would yield upwards of 800 bales, and that much cotton would gross about $100,000. The old house burned in 1938, and a tornado leveled the gin in 1943, but the family withstood those disasters and looked confidently to the future.

By the time the elder Williams died in 1958, his boys were already in command of the farm, and they subsequently divided it up four ways, with each one setting up his own separate farming operation. Ralph, the oldest, got the family home, a brick structure with English Tudor trappings, built on the spot where the original house had stood. All around it now are water oaks and post oaks and magnolias and pecans, massive sentinels planted as much as seventy years ago by the patriarch. The commissary building, a red brick structure with iron bars over the windows, lies in the shade of the biggest oak, and the cotton gin and warehouse are across the road, and a few tenant houses are visible in the distance.

Ralph and Leo, one of his brothers, were in the commissary on a still and humid July morning, and except for them, nobody was around. They were not dressed for work, and there was nothing on the shelves to sell, and there were no clerks and no customers. The single gas pump outside was rusty and inoperative, and weeds grew up around the buildings across the road. Leo was reading the morning paper.

"The biggest thing that's changed here is the damn labor," he said in answer to a question. "We used to have plenty of help, white and colored. Now the government has put everybody on welfare, and that's all the damn nigger wants."

Ralph said something about the Mafia controlling agriculture, and the Jews controlling the food market, and the big companies being in cahoots with the government, and farmers getting sucked into a trap on the soybean market. Leo finished perusing the paper.

"I put a hundred and sixty-five more acres of row crop land into pasture this year," he said. "I used to have some good white people and some good Nigras, tenant farmers, but they quit. There just wasn't enough for both of us to make out on halves. I've been working seven days a week. I never worked as hard as I have the past two or three years."

The two men described life on the farm in the thirties—"We had this store for them, and we financed people to get their own land, and we cut timber and built houses for them, we gave them year-round work"—and how it has changed since then:

"They began leaving when the war started, when they could get higher wages in the war industry, and when they left they'd never come back. And then the government farm programs killed us. The soil bank, paying people not to plant—that put us out of the ginning business. We dropped from two thousand three hundred bales to four hundred bales in one year, and the next year we were out."

"The biggest enemy the farmer has got is the U.S. government," Leo said. "The amount of money they actually spend on farms is damn little. And they're lettin' somebody manipulate the market—the Jews, the Mafia, I don't know who the hell it is. You tell me. All I know is, you could take rat shit and paint it white and sell it for rice, and when it got scarce the price would jump sky high. You get into soybeans and the price goes down. You get into livestock and the price goes down. I'm gettin' out of the hog business. I've got the biggest hog lot in this county—and it ain't nothin'. My two boys help me farm, but I don't want them to come back here and suffer like I have. They might as well let the government feed 'em and pay 'em. If you don't have enough sense to pour piss out of a boot, if you can't find your ass with a pair of deer horns, you can still get the government to take care of you."

Ralph testified to the reality of rising prices. "I bought ten tons of soybean meal last October for a hundred and eighteen dollars a ton," he said, "and before I sold the cows I was feeding it to, seven months later, the same stuff cost me four hundred and twenty dollars a ton. I can show you the feed bill if you don't believe it." Ralph is the oldest of the sons—he is sixty-six—but he married late, and his two boys are still in school at Crenshaw Christian Academy, the white refuge from school desegregation. "What'll I tell 'em when it's time for them to decide what they want to do? I don't know. I'd hate to see this land sit idle, growin' up in scrub oaks and pines. I'd

love for 'em to come back. They might be able to make a living
off livestock."

Leo said a tractor and accessories that cost $1,700 in 1947
would cost $5,000 now, and Ralph said no, it would take at
least $7,000, maybe more. They talked about the weather—a
freak snowstorm last winter, then too much rain, making
spring planting a month late, and then the rain stopped. One of
them said something about President Nixon "unloading a
bunch of wheat and soybeans on Russia and Japan—he took
care of the brokers on that deal," and the other started talking
about "the government giving everything away to sorry sonsa-
bitches that won't work," and then Ralph left to pick up the
only worker still living on his place, an elderly Negro man who
does odd jobs for him. When he had driven away, Leo spoke
about his own labor situation.

"I got two families still livin' on my farm, and one of 'em is
havin' a brick house built for him by the government, and he'll
soon to be gone. Anyway, those two, and my boys, age fourteen
and eighteen, and me—that's it. I hired some thirteen-year-old
boys—the law says that's child labor—and it took two of 'em
to lift a bale of hay." He was standing by the gas pump in
front of the commissary, and he looked out across the lawn
toward Ralph's house. "I've seen mornings when this yard was
full of hands ready to go to work, so many of 'em that you had
to turn some of 'em down. Now there's no help at all. Sure, the
work's not as hard, there's more machinery and all that, but
you can't run a place this big with no help. You start worryin'
sometimes about keepin' a roof over your head and food on the
table.

"The city housewife bitches an' bellyaches about the cost of
meat, but she forgets how many raises her husband has gotten
in the past twenty years. We're just in a hell of a mess, and
God help us if the government takes over the farms. Somebody's gotta do this work, but damn——. I'm bitter, I don't
deny it. I've never had as bad an attitude as I've had this year.

I've just got no desire to produce for Russia and China and Japan, or for welfare loafers. I'm already out of cotton, and in a few years I'll get out of peanuts. I won't ever get into pines— I'm too old to get anything out of that—and I'm gettin' out of hogs. That leaves cattle, and the corn, grain, and silage to feed 'em. It's the only thing I can do on my own. My youngest son is crazy about livestock. He's only fourteen. I hope he'll come back, but I don't know."

Back when the Williamses were cotton farmers and times were flush, they worked hard but lived well and enjoyed life, or so they remember it. But looking back now, they can see at least some of the things that started leading them to their present condition. The New Deal provided some jobs for poor people, victims of the Depression, and got them off the farm. The Williamses were probably glad to see them go; they had too many hungry people anyway. Then the war took men away to fight or to work in the factories in the North. Since then, mechanization and new technological advances and chemicals and fertilizers and crop changes and government farm policies have wrought more changes, and inflation has driven up the cost of feed and equipment, and corporate agribusiness has affected prices and changed the competitive picture. Marketing and distribution practices have changed, and there are more middlemen to share the profits, and profits have shrunk because they haven't kept pace with the rising cost of production. Taxes are higher. And finally, perhaps most importantly for farmers like the Williams brothers, labor has changed. People won't work for a free cabin and food out of the garden and a share of the crop, because they can't subsist on that. When the civil rights movement swept across the South, it may not have elevated the black masses to a new plateau of economic well-being, but it marked the beginning of the end of black docility and submissiveness to white authority, and that was when the white family farmer in the South passed the point of no return.

Leo Williams, in his own way, sees that; he doesn't like it, or think it is as it should be, or even as it had to be, eventually and inevitably, but he sees it: "Non-Southern farmers may have all the other problems we've got, but they don't have that one. They never depended on hired help the way we did. I think the worst thing that ever happened in the South was when they brought slaves over here. You can't put your trust and faith and dependence in niggers. They'll lie to you, and steal from you, and cheat you when they can."

Where does he look for relief, for support, for hope? "I used to look to the government, but after what's happened in the past several years, I have no more faith in the government. It takes a crooked sonofabitch to get anywhere in politics. And judges—whoever's got money can buy and sell 'em like cattle. Wallace, if only he hadn't got shot—I heard him on television the other night, and he was givin' 'em hell again, just like he used to. Him and Kennedy meetin' together up in Decatur, I don't know about that. But I'd damn sight rather have Kennedy and Wallace than to have another Republican. My daddy used to say you'll never see a little farmer prosper under a Republican—and it's sure true now."

Ironically, Leo Williams thinks of himself now as a little farmer—and ironically, he is. What he and his brothers have now may be as big in acres as it was thirty-five years ago, but in population and productivity and prosperity it is small and shrinking.

Leo took off his hat and blotted the sweat on his brow with a shirt sleeve. He fanned away the gnats. It was getting close to eleven o'clock. Under high clouds and haziness, the air felt sticky and oppressively hot. "I gotta go," he said. It would soon be time for dinner. "Come back to see us, y'hear?"

James Kolb is in a different category of Crenshaw County farmers than the Williams brothers. He was one of twelve children in a sharecropper family. The farm he grew up on six miles from Luverne is a forest now. He was forty-four years old

when he bought the forty-one-acre farm he now lives on—
bought it with money he earned working in the North—and he
never had any hope or any desire that his own sons would farm
it after him. Now, at the age of seventy-five, he and his wife
live modestly but comfortably there on a combination of Social
Security payments and what they can grow to sell and eat. And
there is one other important difference between Kolb and the
Williamses: he is black. In south Alabama, that is a burden
and a glory.

He spent the best part of thirty years working in Cleveland
and Detroit and Birmingham and Chicago, and during most of
that time his family stayed back home in Crenshaw County,
where subsistence was not easier, but cheaper. They bought the
farm during the war, and Kolb designed the house that is now
the family place, and his father built it.

His Northern odyssey proved to be an ample substitute for
his limited eighth-grade education. On his first stay in Cleveland he met Marcus Garvey, and for a time he seriously considered following the Garvey movement to Liberia; long after
he gave that idea up, he remained an avid reader and disciple
of such black figures as Garvey, Booker T. Washington, and
Frederick Douglass.

When Kolb came back to the farm to stay in the mid-1950s,
he was fifty-five years old and his five children were almost
grown. Only one of the five still lives in rural Alabama. The
others are all in Ohio; one of his sons is a government employee and the other is an official with the AFL-CIO. "None of
them wanted to stay on the farm," he said. "When I came back
here they was already headed to town. I just hoped I could get
by with some corn and peanuts, and a little bit of cotton, and
some truck farmin'. And I have; I guess I've made out all
right."

Kolb remembers the Williams plantation when it was blan-
keted with cotton: "Just the lint that fell off their trailers goin'
into town was enough to fill several sacks. Mister Jim had at

least eight thousand acres out there. They kept poor whites and blacks always in debt to 'em. Then under Roosevelt some of 'em started movin' off—them public works programs took white boys and black boys and give both of 'em shovels just alike, and that's when the change started. And then there was machines to do the pickin', and the government started this soil bank, payin' people not to produce, and they didn't need old John out there anymore—he wasn't profitable, so they ushered him off the farm, and he was illiterate, and he got lost in the city. The big farmer forgets he threw the hatchet that broke old John's leg, and then he blamed him for limpin'."

Had he been white, James Kolb probably could have concentrated on farming and made a better living for himself and his family, but as a black man, he had more to contend with than crops and the weather. Having enjoyed a degree of freedom in the North, however limited, the oppressiveness of white supremacy in Crenshaw County so angered him that he fought against it at every opportunity, and his audacity made him a marked man. In the late 1940s, on one of his periodic sojourns back home, he succeeded in getting thirteen other blacks and himself registered to vote in spite of threats from the sheriff, and when he moved back to stay in the 1950s, he began a personal campaign against school segregation that culminated more than ten years later in the desegregation of the county's schools.

He was no head-scratching supplicator, to hear him tell it, and that is not hard to believe. Tall and trim, looking younger than his age, he is a magnetic and imposing figure, and he speaks in his south Alabama accent with articulate and deftly phrased directness. "I've been called a meddler and a communist and a troublemaker and a smart-aleck nigger," he says, "but I've never showed 'em fear. When this integration thing started they decided they'd try to make the separate equal. I told 'em, 'To me, segregation is foolish, but if you want it, that's okay with me—just so it's equal. But you been prayin' cream and livin' skim milk, and that won't do.' When two of my grandchildren entered the white school on this freedom of choice thing in 1966, my mailbox was bombed and the Ku Klux painted a big KKK on the highway out in front. The FBI came in, but I told 'em not to stay. My nest was well feathered. I had everything but a machine gun."

As if he didn't have his hands full with white obstacles to his freedom, Kolb has sometimes been bluntly critical of many local blacks, and he has earned a reputation as a man not to be messed with. "Money don't mean nothin' to me," he said. "What I'm interested in is principle. You can't be bought that way. You've got a white power structure to fight here, and a black man too. We've got too many men with a second-grade education who say they've been called to preach. I belong to the Church of Christ, and I'm one hundred percent for the church, but I'm against a lot of its members, in the white church and the black—they're as far from bein' Christians as I am from bein' a white man."

Race relations in Crenshaw County have improved somewhat in recent years—Kolb says he'd have "caught a blue flame" a few years ago for some of the things he freely does now—but in economic terms, the change is hardly noticeable. The only black official in the county is a young man recently appointed to the police force. There are no black clerks in the stores, and none in the courthouse, and school desegregation still operates to the advantage of whites. There is some black employment in the two small apparel factories, but on the farms, where most of the people still live, times are hard for everybody. "The government is drownin' the little man," Kolb says. "You can't make money farmin' around here, whether you're black or white. We're starvin' while Eastland and them are settin' up there drawin'.

"I had a white man tell me one time that when all the niggers that's gone North come back, the houses they used to live in will be gone. He was right—they are. But I told him,

'Don't worry about it—when they come back they'll be speakin' a different language.' And I was right too. The white man used to need the black, and then he thought he didn't. The black man used to need the white too, and now a lot of 'em think they don't. What we're gonna have to come to is an understanding that we need each other. We got to get together."

Getting the black and white farmers of Crenshaw County together—the poor ones, and that means most of them—is an idea that Kolb and a white feed mill owner named G. T. Miller have nursed into budding reality. The two men and their wives have been most instrumental in the formation of the Black and White Co-op, Inc., a membership organization that has collected family dues ($5 a year) from more than 400 Crenshaw Countians and amassed more than $50,000 in gifts and no-interest loans. The co-op is buying a building from Miller, and it has plans to start a grocery, a livestock processing plant, and a canning and freezing plant. Kolb and another black farmer, Jessie Ridgeway, started pushing the co-op idea in 1969; they are now its president and vice-president, and Miller's wife, Clara, is its secretary. About 20 percent of the dues payers are white, but the Millers are the only white family actively involved in the organization's meetings and planning sessions.

The Black and White Co-op is similar to dozens of others that have sprung up in the South in recent years. Its basic objective is to help poor farmers increase their income and improve their living conditions. "Way down South in the heart of Dixie," says a heading on the cover of a planning booklet they have prepared, "Black and White working together for a better America."

If cooperation between blacks and whites seems like an idealistic undertaking in Crenshaw County, the economic rescue of poor farmers seems even more ambitious. There are about 3,500 families living in the county (roughly 30 percent of them black), and of the total, more than 500 are farmers with fewer than 50 acres of land, about 500 have no running water in their homes, fully 2,500 earn less than $3,000 a year, and about 1,000 earn less than $1,000. Even if the co-op can overcome opposition and apathy and inertia, it will take some minor miracles to make agriculture profitable for the masses of farmers there.

But the co-op organizers are undeterred by the magnitude of the task. G. T. Miller, sitting down for noonday dinner in his home near the feed mill, served himself from the platters and bowls of fried chicken, pork chops, field peas, butter beans, corn off the cob, carrots, sliced tomatoes, and biscuits, washed down with large glasses of sweet milk and topped off with a slice of lemon pie, and between bites he talked about the plans for the co-op.

"Any farmer, even a poor one, can have the same things on his table we got here," he said, "and if we get the cannery and the food bank, he can have 'em all year long. We're gettin' together all these facts and figures about our farms and income and all, and we already got a lot of folks to sign up. We got some nice gifts and loans, too, and we're gonna try to get some of that revenue sharin' money. Things are gettin' better—I'd say about forty-five percent better than they used to be. Don't let me do all the talkin'. We're proud to have you come see us. Just make yourself at home. You shoulda brought your family. Hep yourself to some more of those beans."

Miller is a nonstop talker, and for a seventy-four-year-old man he has remarkable energy and stamina. He has a third-grade education, a keen business sense, and an empathy for the poor that is rooted in a firsthand acquaintance with poverty. He is a lifelong resident of Crenshaw County, and his years there have been filled with a fascinating combination of the routine and the unconventional. He has plowed barefooted behind an ox, traveled from Canada to the Gulf Coast by car, served time in a federal penitentiary for making moonshine (barbering Al Capone while he was there), been a member of

the Ku Klux Klan, been beat up by Klansmen for warning a
Negro that he was marked for a flogging, been married three
times, raised four children, and made as much as $35,000 a
year in the feed mill business.

In 1967 he was hit by a boycott when he refused to submit
to a Klan demand that he fire a black employee whose son had
enrolled as a freedom-of-choice transfer in the white school.
His business profit plummeted from almost $28,000 the year
before to $6,000 in 1967, and to a net loss two years hence. He
has never regained his former volume of business—in part
because agriculture in the county has continued to decline—
but a good many of his customers have come back, including
some Klan members, and about fifty of the farmers who boycotted his business (again, including some Klan members)
have now paid dues in the co-op.

There is about Miller a disarming sincerity and simplicity
that disguises his shrewdness as a businessman and his determination as an advocate of racial and economic equality. He is
country as can be, a courteous, religious, patriotic man in bib
overalls who doesn't drink, smoke, cuss, chase women, or use
big words. And he is also a successful merchant who spends
much of his time and money trying to make farming a profitable enterprise for the people of his community.

(He is also a bit eccentric. At the height of the Cuban
missile crisis, he built a 16-cubicle, 64-bed fallout shelter
under his house, and it waits in emptiness now for the day
when H-bombs threaten the peace of Luverne. Gene Williams,
one of Ralph and Leo's brothers, tried to buy one of the
cubicles from him. Miller told him he was free to come and
stay whenever a nuclear attack threatened, but when he said
that "whites would have half the rooms and coloreds would
have the other half," Williams replied that he wouldn't take the
cubicle as a gift under those circumstances. "I told him,"
Miller says, "that if a war ever comes, you'll be the first one
here.")

As a septuagenarian dynamic duo, G. T. Miller and James Kolb have given people around Luverne something to talk about and think about. In their complementary and unorthodox ways, they have probably done more to improve race relations and economic conditions than anyone else in the county. But in spite of their efforts, agriculture remains an occupation with decreasing viability there, and there is only a remote chance that the Black and White Co-op can reverse that decline. Young people are not going into farming. Only three men under thirty-five years of age in the county now make all of their income from farming. Once-prosperous farmers like the Williams brothers now face the future with uncertainty and foreboding. Paradoxically, they may be even more vulnerable than the smaller farmers, because they cannot maintain their former level of operation without a labor force, and the labor is gone. Fate and circumstances and what some would call poetic justice have brought down the once mighty white planter. The moral of his decline, if there is a moral, is not that injustice doesn't pay; it is rather that adversity falls on the just and the unjust. And it is falling now, like a soaking rain, on farmers everywhere.

The crape myrtles and hollyhocks bloom profusely in the sultry July heat. Afternoon thunderstorms drench the brick-red clay and the pines, and leave pockets and patches of fog after dark. The meadows glisten in green and velvety softness under the morning dew. Sharecropper cabins bulge with stored hay like stuffed toys, or sag and sink in the suffocating grasp of the kudzu vines. Crenshaw County, and all of rural America, reads the familiar signs of reassurance and new signs of warning with proper ambivalence. "We're headed somewhere," said James Kolb, "but nobody seems to know exactly where it is."

Family farming is like country cooking and handmade furniture: at its best, it is simple, personal, creative, authentic, even noble—and it is vanishing. As with all the other victims of modernity, the demise of the family farm is at best a mixed blessing, and at worst a tragic loss. War, mechanization, government policies, consolidation, technological research, specialization, marketing, taxes, urbanization, labor, inflation, weather—all have affected or been affected by the changes in agriculture. The net effect of that combination of forces has been to strengthen the hand of the agribusiness conglomerates and to continue the erosion of almost all other farm enterprises, whatever their regional location or size or racial makeup might be. Agriculture as it has traditionally been practiced in this country is now out of phase with the times. Somehow, agriculture seems the poorer for it, and so do the times, and so do we all.

Land : No More Milk and Honey

Since 1959, when Alaska and Hawaii became states, the territory of the United States has remained virtually unchanged, while the population has increased by almost 30 million. The nation's borders with Canada and Mexico have been fixed for over 120 years, and in that time span the population has mushroomed from 25 million to 210 million.

The basic principle controlling those facts is immutable, universal, and starkly simple: People multiply; land does not. The principle also helps to explain—but does not justify— what the people of the United States have done with and to their land, and that story is not one of the noblest chapters of American history. From the time when it was taken from its original possessors, the Indians, to the present time, when it is endangered by a multiplicity of crises, the greatest threat to the territory of the United States has come not from any outside force, but from ourselves.

Even when there was more than enough land for everybody, there was somehow not enough to slake the thirst of men whose desire was to control all of it. It was seized from the Indians by Spaniards and Frenchmen and Englishmen, who then fought among themselves for its domination. After the wars that fixed the new nation's borders had ended, the possessors of the land turned inward upon one another, waging a bitter and bloody civil war to determine whether there would be one nation or two within the territory.

The outcome, of course, was that there would be one nation, and the vanquished South, for reasons of compulsion and choice and pride and prejudice, would be an inferior region of it, almost a separate place, an underdeveloped colony. Now its second-class status has all but diminished, and the Civil War is receding mercifully from the consciousness of most Americans, and the territory of the United States (excepting Hawaii) has not been seriously threatened by war for more than a hundred years.

Still, the nation's land is threatened now—threatened more seriously, perhaps, than ever before—by internal forces that may be beyond anyone's control. It is threatened by the burgeoning population, and its concentration in metropolitan areas; by the innate and inevitable greed of acquisitive and materialistic people; by the advance of technology; by the exploitation and depletion of natural resources; by the self-generating growth of bureaucracy, the increasing power of government, and the corresponding diminution of individual rights; by profound divisions between diverse people on such issues as economic and political equality, cultural survival, and even land reform.

Without fighting any wars of conquest or adding any substantial area to its realm of sovereignty, the United States in this century—in the past quarter-century—has moved steadily closer to a debilitating crisis over the ownership and control and misuse of its land. The crisis manifests itself in many complex and contradictory ways, and it raises some classic conflicts—between the needs of the majority and the rights of the individual, between the use and the preservation of natural resources, between growth and stability, between old values and new necessities. These conflicts arise in every section of the country; if there ever was a distinction to be made between land use and misuse in the South and in the rest of the country, that distinction no longer obtains. As blacks and Appalachian whites and Indians pouring into the cities have discovered— and as middle-class whites fleeing to the suburbs have also learned—there is no Promised Land, no land of milk and honey remote and secure from the manifold problems of society, no place where freedom is available to a chosen few.

There are more than three and a half million square miles of land in the fifty states of the Union—over two and a quarter billion acres. The federal government owns one-third of it— some 760 million acres, including more than 55 million acquired over the years from private owners—and the combined holdings of state and local governments further increase the amount of government-owned property to nearly half of the total. The Indians, who once could claim it all, now have about 50 million acres, and the federal government maintains a substantial degree of supervision and control over most of that.

The bulk of the federally owned land is public domain property, land acquired or claimed by the government west of the Mississippi River well over a century ago. Almost half of eleven Western states, and 97 percent of Alaska, is public land. Agencies of the Department of the Interior—the Bureau of Land Management, the Bureau of Reclamation, the Bureau of Indian Affairs, the Fish and Wildlife Service, the National Park Service—own 539 million acres, over 90 percent of which is in the West. The Department of Agriculture, principally through the U.S. Forest Service, holds title to 187 million acres, and the Department of Defense (Army, Navy, Air Force, Corps of Engineers) owns 30 million acres, leaving less than 4 million acres in the possession of other federal agencies.

These figures exclude an undetermined amount of land which has been given a particular character and a limited use as a direct result of federal initiative. All the land that has been put under water in public lakes and reservoirs, the land acquired for urban renewal, for transmission and power lines, and for federal highways—including more than 3 million acres in the 41,000-mile network of interstates—is in addition to the acreage classified as federally owned. So is the acreage taken up by industries which operate with a heavy federal subsidy—aerospace and transportation, to name just two.

The federal government's stewardship of the land has at times been impressive; our national parks and forests attest to that fact. But with the growth in population and affluence there has been a corresponding increase in appetite and consumption, and now the instances of land abuse by agents of the federal government are increasing in number and in seriousness. Some examples:

• A report on the Bureau of Reclamation issued in 1971 by associates of Ralph Nader accused the agency of building dams and irrigation projects for the benefit of "politicians, bureaucrats and a few profiteering irrigators." In seventy years, the bureau has undertaken almost two hundred major water projects, and it now controls almost 8 million acres of land in nineteen Western states. The Nader report says the bureau has "outlived its usefulness" and should halt its "senseless" damming of the West. The report is specifically critical of the Central Arizona Project, which is aimed at diverting water from the Colorado River to Phoenix and Tucson at an estimated cost of $1.4 billion. Calling it a "boondoggle" and a "raid on the U.S. treasury," the report urges Congress to halt the project. The bureau, the report states, is harming the environment, driving small farmers off the land, providing huge water subsidies to corporate farms, violating Indian water rights, and contributing to salinity problems in Western rivers.

• The U.S. Army Corps of Engineers, a federal agency since 1824, now controls about the same amount of land as the Bureau of Reclamation, but the scope of its operations is vastly greater. The Corps owns land in every state but Utah and Wyoming; it is the custodian of more than 4,000 civil works projects costing in excess of $30 billion; it has altered about 20,000 miles of rivers and waterways with dams, reservoirs, levees, deeper channels, and even new channels. In a 1970 book, *The Diligent Destroyers*, author George Laycock singled out the Corps as the prime destroyer. Their approach, he wrote, runs something like this: "When a river silts up—dredge it. When it runs crooked—straighten it. When it runs straight—deepen it. Where it runs at all—stop it. And where it doesn't run—build a canal." This "public be dammed" attitude, faithfully funded by Congress for decades, now menaces waterways and landscapes in every section of the country.

• The Tennessee Valley Authority, third largest of the federal dam builders, once enjoyed a reputation as the government's most enlightened and progressive public works agency, but in recent years it has aroused more criticism than either of its older and larger sister agencies. In the years after its creation in 1933, TVA survived repeated assaults by private power interests to become the nation's largest producer of electric power and an international symbol of American efficiency. It turned the Tennessee River into an unbroken stairway of navigation lakes, saved countless millions of dollars through flood control, and produced more electricity for more people at lower cost than ever before. Now it is drawing fire for its contributions to strip mining, water pollution, destruction of free-flowing streams, regional development schemes, and manipulation of the real estate market. Late in 1972, a federal court of appeals upheld a lower court decision blocking TVA from further work on the Tellico Dam, a project on a tributary of the Tennessee River that the Environmental Defense Fund had challenged as being in violation of federal laws protecting the environment. TVA is also the world's largest purchaser of surface-mined coal. The Council on Environmental Quality estimates that almost a quarter of a million acres of land were marred by strip mining in 1971, and most of it is not being reclaimed; TVA, as the chief offender, is thus trading its once sterling reputation as a savior of the land and taking on instead a despoiler's image.

• Mismanagement of Indian lands by the Bureau of Indian Affairs has become almost a tradition. So many documented examples of broken treaties fill the record of the federal government's relationship with Indian tribes that the record is now beyond explanation, beyond defense, and beyond redemption.

To these examples can be added scores of cases involving the Departments of Housing and Urban Development, Agriculture, Defense, and Transportation. Urban renewal projects have forced tens of thousands of people from their homes, and replaced only a fraction as many; interstate highways and other road projects have uprooted and divided communities in urban and rural areas alike; policies of the Department of Agriculture have consistently favored the biggest and most powerful landowners at the expense of the poor; and the Army, Navy, and Air Force have military reservations covering 26 million acres—the equivalent of New Hampshire, Vermont, Massachusetts, Connecticut, Rhode Island, New Jersey, and Delaware combined.

For all its usurpation and abuse of the land, though, the federal government is by no means alone. State and local governments have added to the problem in numerous ways, and the activities of corporations and private individuals have also had a devastating effect.

A *Christian Science Monitor* series on the installment land sale business in early 1973 portrayed "a land-management disaster" in an advanced stage. As many as 10,000 companies, from small-scale subdividers of the family farm to mass-sale corporations such as Boise Cascade and ITT, are making the sale of rural land into what is conservatively estimated as a $5-billion-a-year business. Said the *Monitor* series: "Once centered in Florida, where in the 1920s the sale of lots underwater became a national joke, the industry has boomed along with an affluent and mobile American society. The industry's tentacles reach across the nation and even stretch overseas."

The location of new communities is often determined by the availability of land and by the whim of individuals. The effect on such things as the environment, public services, and water supply is seldom considered. Unrestrained developers buy cheap land, cut it into small lots, build a few roads and houses, and make promises about water, electricity, gas, sewers, stores, and paved roads that seldom are kept. Not every such enterprise is a fraud, of course, but greed consistently takes a high toll. Farming is made untenable, purchasers are bilked out of hard-earned savings, the price of land is artificially inflated, environmental problems proliferate. If the investors succeed in the rapid urbanization of rural lands, they bring about a host of problems the new communities are not prepared to deal with; if they create only "paper" towns, they rob gullible individuals who are taken in by false promises. And either way, somebody usually makes a financial killing in the transfer of land titles. The dreams of landless people who want to own a piece of America, of city people who want to have a place in the country, of winter-weary people who want to own a place in the sun, are exploited by entrepreneurs whose dream is to get rich quick. And the result, as often as not, is a multiple disaster.

In every state of the Union, installment land sale developers are in business, but the heaviest market is in the southern half of the country, from California to the seacoast of the Carolinas. It is impossible to separate the legitimate enterprises from the rip-off artists. New towns, subdivisions, shopping centers, resorts, summer home communities, and recreational complexes are booming everywhere, and they run the gamut from the opulent to the tacky, from the creative to the accidental. Some of the projects are cut-and-dried frauds, without any redeeming virtues; others are well-planned and promising attempts to re-create a viable and productive community life. And even in the best of circumstances, serious problems accompany the first bulldozer.

The facelifting now in progress on the American landscape probably cannot be controlled. If government is restrained, private enterprise continues its surgical tinkering; if private interests are limited, government must apply the limitations. And often, it is the combined assault of government and private enterprise which lays waste to the land. It is both private corporations and government agencies at the local, state, and federal levels which have been responsible for the excesses and abuses of urban renewal, public housing, and the interstate highway system. And it is private enterprise, with a strong assist from federal agencies such as TVA, which is responsible for the fact that more than 4 million acres of American land have been strip-mined. For a while, most of that devastation was confined to Appalachia; now, under the impetus of a national "energy crisis," it is shifting to the Western Plains, where nearly a trillion tons of coal lie waiting to be stripped. Most of the land above it belongs to the federal government, to the Crow and Northern Cheyenne Indians, and to the Burlington Northern Railroad. Unless the Indians, farmers, ranchers, conservationists, state elected officials, and others in Montana, Wyoming, and the Dakotas can consolidate their opposition to indiscriminate stripping by the giant energy companies, the Plains may become another Appalachia.

To be against such developments is to be against progress. Who would dare resist the production of enough electric power to satisfy the demands of the American people? Who could be so foolish as to oppose safer highways, or recreational lakes, or slum clearance, or new towns? Who could be against building residential communities on dredged-up coastal land, or second-home subdivisions in the mountains? Certainly not the champions of free enterprise, or the government advocates of growth. Growth is the single most important yardstick by which we measure progress.

So we are growing, and there is no way to turn it off. Environmentalists and conservationists warn us constantly of the consequences, but we go on flooding and paving and subdividing the land, making it beyond restoration. Growth begets growth, and the land diminishes. When it becomes scarce, its desirability increases, its value increases; it is coveted, pursued, hunted, and ultimately it is people with money and power who get it, whether they be private individuals, corporations, or government officials—and getting the land, of course, makes them richer and more powerful, and the landless are made poorer and weaker.

Near the end of 1972, Roy Reed of the New York *Times* reported that between the Civil War and about 1910, the South's former black slaves amassed an estimated 15 million acres of land. Now, the total has been reduced to less than 5 million acres. Migration to the North, the complexities of property ownership, confusion over titles and other legal matters, the assessment of taxes, fraudulent maneuvers, and outright theft have all been instrumental in the decline.

In Appalachia, where landownership has been effectively negated by such legal devices as the broad form deed and the power of eminent domain, mountain residents are victimized by government agencies, coal companies, and resort developers alike. Tom Gish, a newspaper editor in the Kentucky mountains, said in a speech in 1972 that this triple threat is "out to do away with the mountain man and all that he represents." He continued:

Oh, they are not going to take us out and shoot us. They are out to change us into something else: the homogenized all-American model American. Or, if they can't change us, then they want to force us to move from the mountains altogether. No mountain resi-

dents, no mountaineers, no mountain poverty, no problems. . . .
There are numerous things wrong with mountain living for many,
indeed for most, mountain people. It is not pleasant to be poor. Our
one great need is for money—an adequate economic base, so we
can have proper food, housing, clothing, and meet our basic health
and other essential needs. No one has yet come up with an answer
to the economic problems. We keep having coal and tourism
thrown at us, but we all know what coal does to the man and to the
soil, and tourism displaces and dehumanizes the mountain man just
the same as the coal mines. . . . Had we asked the right questions
and insisted upon the right answers at the right time, we might
have been saved from a TVA that devastates an entire area for its
strip coal, from a Corps of Engineers that builds dams simply to
build dams, from a Forest Service that serves only the lumber industry, from an Appalachian Regional Commission that seeks not
to assist, but to eliminate, an entire culture rich in its own heritage.
We might even have been saved from our own folly in turning over
the greatest wealth in the nation to a few moneymen from the outside who wanted our minerals.

Black nationalists of the Republic of New Africa speak of
building an independent black nation somewhere in the South.
Young Mexican Americans—Chicanos—have rallied around
Aztlan, a vast region stretching from California to Texas which
was settled by their ancestors and ceded to the United States in
1848 after the war with Mexico. Indians occupied Alcatraz
Island and seized the town of Wounded Knee, South Dakota,
to symbolize their demands for justice from the white man.
These are audacious acts in the eyes of many people, including
many blacks and Chicanos and Indians. Yet every man who
has been dispossessed can feel a kinship with those men,
whether or not he agrees with the particular methods they
choose to express their outrage.

Conflicts over land are as old as history. The complexities of
modern society intensify those conflicts, bringing into conten-
tion principles and ideas which often seem to have equal
merit: individual rights versus the public welfare, the conve-

58

nience of the city versus the freedom of the open spaces, private enterprise versus government regulation, property rights versus the power of eminent domain, stability versus growth. The poor of all races are driven from the rural countryside, or flee from it, only to be confined by racial and economic discrimination in the decaying ghettos of the cities; affluent people flee the city in search of peace and comfort and safety, and their destination is often the same rural countryside the poor have been forced to leave; the germs of poverty and the germs of materialism thus breed in a continuous cycle of creation and decay and regeneration. In this process, land is a commodity, a thing to be bought or sold or stolen. But land is also a resource; its supply is limited, and it cannot be reproduced. It has meaning and value beyond any monetary measurement. The destruction of that meaning and that value, whether by government agencies or private corporations or individual citizens, is a grave and irredeemable act. It is also a common act in contemporary America.

In 1963 the federal government took the first steps toward development of a national recreation area in a remote region of western Kentucky and Tennessee. Ostensibly, the government conceived of its initiative as an act of stewardship; it looked upon the land as a natural resource to be conserved for the perpetual benefit and enjoyment of millions of Americans. But in its actions—particularly in its treatment of the people who lived on the land—it seemed to regard the region as a mere commodity, a territory to be taken by superior strategy, the way military logistics experts plan the capture of a territorial objective.

The Tennessee Valley Authority was the agency assigned to develop the project, and on the surface, it appeared to be a good choice. When it was created forty years ago, TVA was unique. Headquartered in Knoxville, in the midst of the people it was intended to serve, it was a federal agency where the action was, a government department devoted to flood control

and navigation and production of electric power and conservation of natural resources, a supplier of human services in a
region desperately needing those services. It was something
good happening in the South, something promising and excep-
tional. It was doing for people what they could not do for
themselves: providing the might and the money to make
nature work for the benefit of the population.

But by the time TVA began its development of the national
recreation area, it was also doing in its region what the Bureau
of Reclamation does in the West, and what the Corps of Engineers does all over the country: contributing to the exploitation of the land and its people. For TVA, land had become a
commodity.

> Oh, the stars are shining and the meadow is bright
> But under the trees is dark and night
> In the land between the rivers.
>
> —Robert Penn Warren,
> "The Ballad of Billie Potts"

The land jabs northward out of Tennessee like the wrinkled
thumb of a giant, stretching forty miles from knuckle to nail
and spreading five to ten miles thick between the jagged shore-
lines of Kentucky Lake and Lake Barkley. There is archaeo-
logical evidence that human beings lived there seven centuries
ago. It was Shawnee Indian country until white pioneers from
North Carolina came on flatboats in the 1790s, and for 175
years after that, the immigrants and their posterity farmed and
hunted and dug iron ore and cut timber and made whiskey in
that isolated section of western Kentucky and Tennessee. For
most of those years the region was known as the Land Between
the Rivers, for there were no dams then, and the Tennessee
and Cumberland rivers flowed unchecked on their northerly
course to a confluence with the Ohio. In its heyday half a
century ago, the Land Between the Rivers was home for almost
10,000 people. It was a distinctive place, a wooded isthmus of
hills and hollows and bottomland set apart from the surround-

60

ing countryside by the rivers (they were not bridged until the 1930s), and its very isolation nourished and embellished the mixture of truth and myth that formed the history of the land and its people.

Now it is called the Land Between the Lakes, and all the people are gone. They have been uprooted and removed by the TVA, which has turned the area into a vast outdoor playground, a public recreation center covering almost 200,000 acres. TVA calls it "a national demonstration in maximum use of available resources for outdoor recreation and conservation education." The word "conservation" in that context is sadly ironic, for almost nothing that was characteristic of the region or its people has been conserved. The Land Between the Lakes is a "national demonstration" of the destructive consequences of bureaucratic insensitivity and greed, an example of cold and impersonal manipulation to create a controlled environment in which the past is obliterated and all human activity is regulated. It is the concept of urban renewal writ large across a rural landscape. Robert Penn Warren's poetic and prophetic lines, written more than a quarter of a century ago, are now an epitaph for the Land Between the Rivers.*

* I have been personally involved on three levels in the controversy between TVA and the people of the Land Between the Rivers: as a journalist, as a property owner, and as a litigant in federal court. Several times over the years, I have written about the region for magazines and newspapers. In 1963 I bought 130 acres of land in the area with my wife, a native of the region whose family had lived there for four generations. Three months after we bought the land, it was announced that TVA would develop an outdoor recreation project in the area, and six months later, TVA revealed for the first time its intention to purchase all of the private acreage to supplement the government's already substantial holdings. Along with some of the residents, we refused to sell our land, and TVA brought condemnation proceedings against us. The legal question we raised was whether TVA had statutory authority to condemn the land for recreational use. The district and appeals courts ruled in favor of TVA, and in 1972, eight years after the dispute started, the U.S. Supreme Court, with Justice William O. Douglas dissenting, denied our petition for a writ of certiorari. The compensation TVA subsequently made to my wife and me for the property we owned multiplied our original investment in it several times over.

TVA first came to the area more than thirty years ago, to build Kentucky Dam on the Tennessee River. The lake created by that project inundated thousands of acres of river bottom farmland, but it also brought electric power, and it improved navigation, and it put an end to floods above the new water line. Twenty years later, the Corps of Engineers built a similar dam on the Cumberland River and a canal connecting the two lakes, and the land between them became an inland peninsula.

Several federal agencies, as well as many private entrepreneurs, were attracted by the development potential of the region, and in 1959, before the completion of Barkley Dam, the government agencies began informal discussions on its possible uses. The National Park Service was one of those bodies, and in April of 1961 it issued a report recommending federal action to preserve and protect the area from "uncontrolled commercialization and misuse." The report also indicated that not all of the privately owned land in the area would be needed for development—almost half the total acreage was already in federal hands—and it recommended that "certain portions of the entire peninsula area" be excluded from the boundaries of any federal development project that might be undertaken. Later that same year, TVA submitted a report proposing that the government develop a "Between the Lakes National Recreation Area." TVA made no mention of any land acquisition.

No action was taken on the proposals for almost two years. In March 1963, Secretary of the Interior Stewart Udall suggested to President Kennedy that TVA be authorized to implement its proposal. Udall said TVA "has authority to set up and conduct demonstration projects in resource development and to acquire lands needed for such projects," whereas the Park Service would need specific authorization from Congress to become engaged. Three months later, Kennedy signed an executive order giving TVA the job, and a supplemental budget request was sent to Congress.

It took six months for the first appropriation to be passed, and during that time, TVA officials painted a glowing image of the project. Aubrey J. Wagner, chairman of the agency's three-man board of directors, predicted that 4 million to 5 million visitors would be using the area for recreation within three years. He said it would take five years to implement TVA's plans, and he estimated the cost would be about $33 million. Nothing was said about land acquisition.

In January 1964, as soon as the first appropriation cleared Congress, TVA announced for the first time its intention to acquire every acre of land in the area, from the canal connecting the two lakes on the north to U.S. Highway 79 on the south—with the unexplained exception of an aggregate of about 6,000 acres in the southeast corner, adjacent to the town of Dover, Tennessee. Since federal agencies held title to almost 100,000 acres—most of it in a game refuge operated by the Fish and Wildlife Service—the TVA announcement meant that about 100,000 acres of privately owned land would be bought, and about 3,000 people would be dispossessed.

Up to that point, the proposed project had been widely endorsed by public officials in Kentucky and Tennessee, and by most of the residents of the area. But the announcement that all their land would be taken caused a shock wave, and protests were quickly raised. In one form or another, that resistance continued for more than eight years. TVA was given possession of the land by the federal courts, but appeals were pursued on about a hundred parcels of property, and they were not exhausted until 1972. It took 278 invocations of the power of eminent domain and finally, in one case, the help of federal marshals, to clear the land of its people.

Some of them wanted to leave. Like others before them, they had seen the fertile farmlands in the river bottoms inundated by the lakes, seen how unproductive the soil on the ridges was, seen that their best chance to earn a living was not there but somewhere else. And even before that, before the lakes were created, the Land Between the Rivers was in decline, losing people to the larger towns and cities where new industries offered hope for a better life. Other people were less eager to leave, but they had been forced by the government to move before, had fought it and lost, and this time they were resigned with stoic fatalism to the inevitability of it. Still others, dissatisfied with the price they had been offered for the land, followed the laborious trail of legal appeals which sometimes brought them more money, and then finally settled and left.

But a few of them—perhaps fifty families in all, the possessors of most of the tracts of contested land—would not surrender. The issue with most of them was not money—they were saying that no amount of money would compensate them for what they had—but TVA's response was that every man has his price. "They just think they can get more money than what we offer them, that's what it boils down to," one member of the TVA board of directors said of the holdouts. "We think most of them, when it becomes so obvious that they're isolated, they'll eventually find that they want to move out, when there's nobody left around."

So it came down to that: TVA against fifty families. It was a vastly uneven match from the beginning, and as time wore on, the question was not whether they would leave, but when. In the eight-year struggle, the people were not just driven out— they were alienated and embittered. TVA's handling of the exodus was marred time and time again by duplicity and deceit. Officials who professed to be "completely sympathetic" with the problems faced by the landowners, who promised to "do all we can to make the situation less difficult for those whose property is purchased," were the same officials who sanctioned unfair and inconsistent purchasing procedures, who accused landowners of being speculators whose only interest was gouging the government, who helped turn friends and even families against one another. Some people were threatened. Others were bought off.

The local governments of Trigg and Lyon counties, in which the Kentucky portion of the area is located, passed resolutions opposing further land acquisition by TVA except from those owners who wanted to sell, and some of Kentucky's delegation in Congress—most notably Senator John Sherman Cooper—protested TVA's "neglect of the rights of a large number of area citizens," but opposition from Tennessee officials was muted and perfunctory. TVA constantly promised that the communities surrounding the area would reap great economic benefits from the project, and in time the politicians and businessmen and newspapers lost whatever interest they had had in the plight of the area residents and joined in the chorus of TVA's boosterism song. Each year, delegations of residents from between the lakes went before House and Senate appropriations committees to plead for relief, and each year TVA was told to get its house in order, but funds were never withheld. Meanwhile, speculative activities flourished all around the Land Between the Lakes—including the development of a subdivision in the area near Dover that had been excluded from the project—and TVA encouraged these.

The landowners took their case into federal court, where they raised a basic question: Why is it necessary to take our land? They acknowledged that TVA's land acquisitions in the past, however disruptive they had been, were grounded in necessity: the objectives of controlling floods, improving navigation, and creating electricity were sound and essential. The new objective—recreation—seemed almost frivolous by comparison. Why could the government not develop a recreation area on the land it already had? They questioned TVA's authority under the law to use the power of eminent domain for any purpose not related to navigation, flood control, or electric power production. TVA first responded that its authority came from Section 22 of the TVA Act, a sort of Catch-22 paragraph which empowers the agency to conduct "studies, experiments and demonstrations." But that section makes no mention of recreation and does not deal with the question of eminent domain. Later, TVA asserted that its authority derived from President Kennedy's executive order and from subsequent appropriations by Congress—in other words, it claimed de facto authority to do whatever Congress gave it money to do. The courts ultimately agreed with that assertion.

But before they did, TVA spent twice as much as it had estimated it would spend, took twice as long to develop the project, and attracted only one-third as many annual visitors as it had predicted. The agency had said in the beginning that it would develop the project as a "demonstration" and then turn it over to another government agency to operate, but the longer it stayed the less it said about leaving.

These discrepancies served only to heighten suspicions about TVA's intentions, and in that atmosphere of distrust, rumors abounded. Mineral explorations were said to be under way, sites were said to be pinpointed for future industrial development, a planned community like Columbia, Maryland, was said to be on the drawing boards. Large landholdings in and near the between-the-lakes area belonged to some national corporations—including the Kerr-McGee Oil Company, once an economic interest of Oklahoma's late Senator Robert Kerr —and much conjecture centered on those holdings. When Kerr's long-time administrative assistant, Donald McBride, was named in 1966 to a nine-year term on the TVA board of directors, the news was received by some area residents as proof that something big was about to happen. So far, nothing has.

During the years when it was buying up the land, TVA opened a new campsite here, a conservation center there, did a little road work, took over management of the wildlife refuge, and waited for time and impatience and death and economic necessity to take its toll on the diminishing group of holdout landowners. The toll was heavy and inexorable. As the number of owners selling voluntarily or through coercion increased, the pressure on those who remained grew heavier. Stores closed, and service stations; distances between neighbors lengthened; churches moved, or disbanded; people who felt the economic squeeze often could find work only with TVA—and only if they agreed to sell their land. Physical and psychological isolation grew. The months became years, the charges of speculation continued, incidents between landowners and TVA representatives increased. And finally, TVA got the land.

By 1972, the possession was complete except for one frame house, where a disabled veteran of World War II lived alone. On his front porch, a sign was nailed. It was printed in heavy black letters, and it read:

U.S. Property

PENALTY FOR STEALING

The theft of United States Property
of any kind is punishable
by a maximum fine of

$10,000

OR BY

IMPRISONMENT FOR TEN YEARS

OR BOTH

U.S. CRIMAL CODE
18 U.S.C. SECTION 641

The emptying of the Land Between the Lakes helped to reduce the population of all three affected counties in the 1970 census. And Trigg County, which had almost 300,000 acres in 1930, was reduced to half that size, having surrendered land for seven different federal and state projects in forty years.

In the vast acreage of the Land Between the Lakes, TVA in 1971 had a grand total of 75 full-time employees to take the place of 3,000 residents. Tourists do come, of course, to camp and hike, to swim and sail and fish in the waters of the two lakes. Their numbers will multiply as the years pass and the demand for outdoor recreation land increases. But the ones for whom the land was home are gone, taking their memories with them, and leaving behind only cemeteries to mark their former presence.

There is a stillness on the land. Along the narrow creekstone roads, the winter landscape is etched in myriad shades of brown—sedge grass and bullweed stalks, barren trees on a carpet of fallen leaves, decaying shells of unpainted houses staring blankly through vacant windows. Here and there a touch of green breaks the pattern: a cedar tree, a patch of winter rye, a canebrake, a clump of moss. The creeks run clear and frisky after a rain, and there is ice on the blue-gray waters at the ends of the bays. Little changes except the capricious sky, deep blue and cloudless one day, gray and heavy as pewter the next. The only visible sign of life is on the wing— cardinals, bluejays, thrushes, bluebirds, mockingbirds, and more rarely, an owl, a hawk, an eagle, a wild turkey. Only the birds and the wind break the silence.

In the hour it takes to drive the 48 miles of paved road running north and south atop the ridges, a dozen cars might be seen, and on the backwoods roads it is possible to drive for hours without meeting a single traveler.

In summer, cars pulling boats and campers move along U.S. Highway 68, the only east-west road through the area, and there is a bustle of activity at the half-dozen campgrounds TVA has developed, but only an occasional car disturbs the quiet along the back roads. When the sound of the motor has faded and the beige patina of dust has settled on the weeds that press up to the road, a possum may amble across, or a white-tail deer. In the meadows and fields where grain and tobacco once grew, goldenrod and Queen Anne's lace fight a losing battle with thistles and milkweed. Withered cornstalks stir in the breeze, and the sound they make is like soft rain on a tin roof. There is a rose hue on the sumac bushes—the first sign of approaching fall—and the sycamore leaves, turning amber and crinkly in the dry heat, rustle in the wind like tambourines.

No trace can be found of the little crossroads communities that once thrived, places with names like Energy, Wildcat, Turkey Creek, Pleasant Valley. Golden Pond, the largest town, had a bank and a hotel, doctors and lawyers, mills and stores and saloons and cafés, fifty years ago. Only a historical marker stands there now. The mailboxes are long since gone, and the names they bore—Higgins, Oakley, Colson, Wallace, Wilson—remain only on the tombstones. The dead are scattered in cemeteries large and small, in deserted churchyards and forgotten arbors lost under the leaves of a century of autumns. Marked with marble headstones and limestone rocks, they tell their own story. One tombstone, handmade of concrete, bears two words etched in its face: "The Unknown." Another, a marble slab, spells a family name in raised letters, a name that seems to speak for all the land and its people. The name is DOOM.

In the middle of the nineteenth century, massive smelting furnaces were built to extract iron from the plenteous deposits of hematite ore that lay near the surface of the hills between the rivers. Some of the mills employed more than a hundred men, among them Chinese laborers—said to be among the first ever brought to the United States—and Negro slaves. An Irishman named William Kelly discovered the cold-air process for turning iron into steel at a furnace near there in 1850, and six years later an Englishman named Henry Bessemer, with the invention he allegedly stole from Kelly, was on his way to fame and fortune, his name given to the process that built the giant steel mills of Pittsburgh and Birmingham. The furnaces are gone now; only the crumbling stack of Center Furnace and one or two others still stand, fenced in to protect them from souvenir seekers. On the hillsides lay scattered bits of the blue hematite ore, vestiges of the days when the furnaces roared and the mingled sweat of black and white and yellow men flowed freely.

The homesteads of the dispossessed—the barns, the fences, the houses—are buried in undergrowth or gone altogether, most of them either moved by their former owners or bulldozed into holes by TVA, literally swept from the landscape. The only evidence that houses ever stood may be an apple tree, a weeping willow, a walnut, a sugar maple—or the bricks of a fallen chimney, strewn among the weeds like a child's building blocks. Occasionally, a cistern can be uncovered to toss echoes back out of its clammy blackness.

On two occasions after the exodus from the Land Between the Rivers was past reversing—once in March of 1969 and again in May of 1970—some of the people who had been forced to leave came back to commemorate the land. The first time, they gathered in an old church in the former community of Sardis, bringing with them symbolic offerings to be placed in a time capsule. The symbols included an arrowhead—"for the Indians who lived here first"—a piece of hematite ore, a vial of water from the two rivers, a chevron in memory of war victims, a Bible, and a sprig of evergreen, "repesenting eternal life and perennial growth." Two other items were also placed in the small wooden box before it was buried in the cemetery outside the church. One was a purse containing thirty pieces of silver, "to symbolize our betrayal." The other was a copy of the Fourth Amendment to the U.S. Constitution, which says in part: "No person shall be . . . deprived of life, liberty, or property, without due process of law; nor shall private property be taken for public use without just compensation."

The second gathering was to unveil the historical marker in memory of the town of Golden Pond. Its post office was still standing then, and Wilson's General Store—artifacts of rural America. Golden Pond was once like all country towns, and like none of them, a place both typical and unique. It had its own character, its great events, its triumphs and tragedies, its good and bad people living out their lives in anonymity or notoriety. Then it was nothing, not even a ghost town. It was simply gone. There were speeches and eulogies at that last gathering, words of grief and prayer, and a preacher named Will Campbell from Mt. Juliet, Tennessee, was there with his guitar, picking and talking through a song-narrative he had written called "Still Water of Golden Pond." In it were these words:

Long ago we should have known, perhaps as long ago as when we came, for others have traveled the road we travel now. Perhaps the Shawnee braves and their ladies stood huddled together, even as we, hopelessly and helplessly leaving their mark, so that some-one might someday say, "What do these stones mean, these flint-rocks and mounds and arrowheads protruding from the earth?" Perhaps the taking of our land is the final act of judgment for those whose land we took.

But since we knew not, we can now remind the taker of the fire next time. This too will pass away and still others will come—in search of freedom, freedom to breathe, perhaps—will come and reclaim it, drain it, plant it, live it, love it, bear their young, bury their dead.

On one occasion when the landowners went before a Senate appropriations subcommittee to plead for relief, they presented sworn statements from more than seventy former residents who charged TVA representatives with harassment, threats, and lies. They documented the physical and mental suffering of scores of people. The Louisville *Courier-Journal* recorded some of those statements, and a reporter for the paper, William Greider, wrote of them:

Some of the complaints are sensational. Some are petty. Some are simply melancholy accounts of the trauma involved when one gives up a cherished home to make way for progress. No doubt, the statements include exaggerations or misrepresented facts or honest misunderstandings induced by strong emotions.

But taken as a whole, these accounts of personal anguish have an authentic ring to them. The words are those of simple people who have been hurt, deeply. Reading through case after case, the inescapable conclusion is that not all of these people could be confused by their emotions, not all of them could be exaggerating.

In sum, their testaments form a chilling documentary of how government, acting with the best of intentions, can abuse little people.

Another reporter, Frank Ritter of the Nashville *Tennessean,* told of the eviction of George Conroy Atwood, one of the last of the holdouts, in November of 1970. Atwood had ignored an order by a federal judge directing him to appear in court to show cause why he should not be held in contempt for refusing to move. "We had heard that Atwood was a violent man who had threatened to shoot anyone who came on his property," a TVA representative told Ritter.

U.S. marshals were sent to arrest Atwood, and they found him waiting, ready to accompany them peacefully. He was taken to jail pending a hearing, but the judge later released him after Atwood promised not to return to the Land Between the Rivers. Ritter noted that Atwood's future plans were uncertain, and he added: "What is certain is that the way of life which Atwood knew in the Land Between the Lakes when it was populated by people and families and churches and communities is dead. And few, if any, will know—whatever may be the benefits of the parkland for millions of Americans from now on—what a personal tragedy it all is for George Atwood."

Stories like that cut no ice at TVA headquarters. In fact, if the views of the agency's chief solicitor, Thomas A. Pedersen, are at all representative, the belief prevails that TVA, and not the landowners, has been maligned. When Ritter called Pedersen for a comment on Atwood, the solicitor drew on forty years of experience with TVA to conclude that the entire controversy in the Land Between the Lakes had been totally misrepresented in the press. "The story of these people has been told to the point of nausea," he said. "There ought to be some point where reporters would tell things as they are instead of indulging in a lot of sentimental drip. The basic thing here is that Atwood did not obey a federal district judge's order when given every opportunity to do so. I have no sympathy for him. The judge had no other alternative but to arrest the man."

Pedersen said he saw a parallel between people like Atwood and those who show disrespect for the law by rioting or engaging in acts of civil disobedience. "I'm not a hard law-and-order man," he added, "but I don't think you can ignore the courts with impunity. These people who were in the Land Between the Lakes—who claim to be such good citizens—where is their respect for the law? Their respect for the courts? The rights of others? These resisters are a hard-core group . . . as tough a bunch as I've ever seen—a group who felt they were above the law . . . troublemakers, thieves, and moonshine makers."

And as for TVA, Pedersen saw its responsibility this way: "We are not the Red Cross. We are not the welfare department. We are not the man's family. We are the TVA, working at the direction of the President and Congress. We do what we are required to do under the law."

It is all so simple. We do what we are told. The people are not our responsibility. They are troublemakers, thieves, moonshiners, lawbreakers. It has all been said before, done before, a thousand times—the facile stereotyping, the demagoguery, the appeals to law and order. Indians know that, blacks know it, Jews know it, Chicanos know it, the poor of Appalachia know it—and now the former residents of the Land Between the Rivers know it. The people who run TVA, who work for it, are not all villains, not vicious men. Most of them are no doubt decent and sensitive people, fallible human beings like us all. And like most of us, they are loyal—they follow orders, they go by the book, they do not let doubts and questions get in the way of duty. And somehow, the pattern becomes fixed: A conflict arises. Both sides cannot win. Something, somebody, has to give. There is a need for the Land Between the Lakes recreation area. Open space in America is diminishing. Conservation is important, the environment is important, ecology is important. Places must be set aside to relieve the pressure in the cities.

TVA apparently saw the Land Between the Lakes project as an opportunity for the agency to polish its tarnished image. The praise it had earned in earlier years for its enlightened pursuit of the public interest had been eroded by its complicity in strip mining, in water and air pollution, in land speculation. Here was a chance to champion the cause of environmental protection and conservation. The Land Between the Lakes *was* a good idea, and TVA could develop it as well as any government agency.

So the decision was made. But old habits are hard to break. TVA had become too enchanted with its own power, too greedy, too self-righteous, too mendacious. It had become too much like the Corps of Engineers and the Bureau of Reclamation. What began as a farsighted and intelligent project ended up trampling on the rights of a few people with no political leverage. It is an impressive recreational area, enjoyed by tens of thousands of visitors each year, but its impressiveness is sullied by what it cost in human terms.

The pervasive malaise of so many Americans today seems somehow tied to a feeling of rootlessness. Family ties are weaker, the past is irretrievable, the future seems uncontrollable, if not unattainable. Identity is the holy grail, the precious thing all seek but few find, and the sense of community is lost and lamented. One of the most striking things about the people who used to live in the Land Between the Rivers was that so many of them believed they had those things. They had a sense of belonging, a sense of place. No doubt their remembrance of it is mellower than the truth—it was not an easy place to make a living, and nobody got rich there, and many people suffered real hardships—but it was their land, and they cannot replace it.

The tragedy is that the recreation area could have been developed without forcing the people to leave against their will. TVA, from the beginning, was unwilling to compromise. It could have bought only from willing sellers; it could have limited private commercial development, or prohibited it altogether; it could have tried to work out cooperative zoning regulations; it could have made the people an integral part of the environmental protection plan; it could have allowed those who wanted to stay to retain lifetime possession of their homes. In a dozen ways, it could have recognized and supported the basic needs and desires of the people, without affecting the development of the park. What it lacked was the willingness, the desire, to protect the rights of those who wanted to retain a sense of place.

TVA's promotional literature says, "Man's ingenuity and resourcefulness have given new qualities to this once unspectacular land." The Land Between the Lakes is billed as "one of the newest and most exciting outdoor recreation areas in America." The words reverberate with irony: It's a nice place to visit, but you wouldn't want to live there.

And now, at last, nobody does. Under the trees is dark and night in the Land Between the Rivers.

Education: Here Come de Facto

Oliver Brown never became a central figure in the national controversy over school desegregation, but his name ended up on one of the best-known and most significant cases ever decided by the U.S. Supreme Court. *Brown* v. *Topeka* was one of five cases consolidated by the court for its 1954 decision outlawing public school segregation.

It was an anomaly, an accident of history, that Oliver Brown and the state of Kansas came to symbolize the most complex and intractable domestic problem in American history. Brown was not a crusader, and Kansas is not a Southern state, yet the Supreme Court decision set in motion a civil rights crusade that was focused on the South for more than a decade. But in retrospect they may be appropriate symbols after all: with the twentieth anniversary of the *Brown* decision near at hand, segregation and inequality in education—the issue Oliver

75

Brown raised—is still unresolved, and it is no longer a Southern problem, but a national one.

Before Brown died in 1961, black children had begun to enter previously all-white schools in some Southern states, in spite of massive and at times violent white resistance. Kansas and most of the other non-Southern states where segregation had been sanctioned by law had complied with the court's ruling, and the moral and legal pressure of an aroused nation was being brought to bear on the die-hard South. He lived to see a revolution in the making, and to be proud of the small part he played in it.

If he could somehow return now to review the panorama of events in school desegregation since 1961, Oliver Brown would probably be overcome by confusion, bewilderment, and ambivalence. Topeka's schools are less desegregated now than Tampa's, and Wichita's less than Waco's. There is something called de facto segregation, not to be confused with de jure segregation; the latter is said to be dead, but the former thrives. The schools of the South are substantially more desegregated than those of other regions, but the schools in Atlanta and New Orleans and several other Southern cities have essentially the same problems of segregation and inequality as the schools of Boston and Philadelphia and Detroit. There has been organized resistance to school integration by Chinese citizens in San Francisco, white "ethnics" in Brooklyn, and white "Middle Americans" in Pontiac, Michigan. Non-Southern cities from Rochester to Pasadena have rediscovered segregation, attempted to eliminate it, and found themselves thwarted by phenomena known as "white flight" and "white backlash." In Jackson, Mississippi, where advocacy of integration was once considered tantamount to treason, the local chamber of commerce has conducted a major campaign to encourage support for integrated public schools. Hardly anybody openly advocates school segregation anymore, but there is massive support for "freedom of choice" and "neighborhood

schools," and the choices people make and the neighborhoods
they live in tend almost invariably to be segregated. The same
kind of school bus Oliver Brown's daughter once had to ride to
a segregated school now takes some children long distances to
integrated schools, and a move is afoot in Congress to make
such busing unconstitutional. A large number of congressmen
and senators from the North who once assailed the South for
its segregated ways are now outspokenly resistant to integration, especially when it involves busing. George Wallace, probably the most famous segregationist the South has produced in
this century, won the Democratic presidential primary in
Michigan by railing incessantly against the use of buses to
desegregate schools. Appreciable numbers of blacks have become opponents of busing and of school integration. Desegregation in many places has resulted in the closing of formerly
all-black schools and the demotion or dismissal of thousands of
black teachers and administrators. The federal courts have
generally moved further in the direction of school integration,
but litigation continues, and no end is in sight. Two U.S.
Presidents, Kennedy and Johnson, supported school integration, and Johnson in particular put the weight of his administration behind it, but a third President, Nixon, has pushed in
the opposite direction. Social scientists have assembled data
which purport to show that school integration is variously
beneficial to blacks, harmful to them, helpful to whites, damag-
ing to them, an asset to everybody, and of no consequence to
anybody. The performance of teachers and administrators of
both races in desegregated schools has ranged from inspiring
and heroic to incompetent and shabby. And the students, black
and white, Southern and Northern, have manifested almost
every conceivable response to desegregation; they have become fast friends and allies, they have ignored one another,
they have been estranged and aloof and hostile. Oliver Brown
could certainly be excused for not knowing what to make of it
all. In a sense, he has missed everything—and then again, he

has missed nothing. The white South has lost its fight to preserve the dual school system, and the North has been divested of its moral self-righteousness, but all over the nation —and in metropolitan areas especially—segregation and inequality of educational opportunity are still widespread and persistent.

Oliver Brown lived through part of the first generation of school desegregation, a period that ended, coincidentally or not, at about the time Richard Nixon became President of the United States. It was a time of violent resistance in the South: segregationists determined to maintain white supremacy clashed with abolitionists committed to the eradication of segregation. The integrationists had an initial goal that was simple and direct: they wanted black and white teachers and children to be together in the same schools, so they could get the same basic educational preparation for life in a free and open American society. Many of them had faith that desegregation per se—the moving of bodies—would accomplish that goal. The segregationists undoubtedly believed that too, and feared it; they devoted themselves to a defense at all costs of the way of life that assured them, as white people, of privilege and supremacy and advantage.

By the late 1960s, the abolitionists had achieved victory on paper. Segregation as a philosophical article of faith had been deflowered, dual school systems were falling all across the South, and biracial schools had become commonplace. But the first generation was only a prelude. It ended the most obvious manifestations of de jure segregation, it placed the South under essentially the same legal imperatives as the rest of the country, and it brought about changes in the actual assignment of children that in time advanced the South to a level of desegregation that generally had not been reached in other regions. And yet, what the integrationists hoped for and the segregationists feared did not come to pass: the demise of segregation, where it took place, did not bring about equality;

on the contrary, it often resulted in increased strife and tension and in an unabated continuation of discrimination. Furthermore, it often led to a white exodus to segregated suburban school systems, or to private schools, and the resulting resegregation took on a form long familiar in the North. It was called de facto segregation—a consequence, supposedly, of private initiative rather than public law—and as time passed, more and more white Southerners, particularly in urban areas, began to say that their schools were no different from those in the North, and to insist that the courts treat them the same way.

The distinction between de jure and de facto segregation, and between the South and the rest of the country, has become so blurred as to be meaningless. In the South and out of it, court suits have been brought against school segregation, and in dozens of cities, judges have ordered desegregation to proceed, often necessitating the use of buses to transport children. As a consequence, desegregation and busing have become national concerns, and public opinion polls have shown a remarkable consistency from region to region in the reactions of people to these issues. Busing has been a welcome and fully accepted fixture on the American school scene for more than fifty years, and it was never seriously opposed until desegregation entered the picture, but now it is objected to by about three-fourths of the population. The bus is no longer just a mechanical means of getting children to and from school; it is also the last in a long line of techniques that have been used to end racial isolation, and it is clearly an essential tool in that process. A wide variety of people—from avowed white racists to black separatists to elitist intellectuals to class-conscious suburbanites to people who simply don't want to be inconvenienced—have been joined in opposition to the use of that tool, and for the most diverse individual and collective reasons, they have arrived at a similar conclusion: Integration as it has been attempted does not work, and segregation is not a sufficiently critical problem to make its elimination imperative.

That is the prevailing national mood. Where desegregation is in being—and there is still a substantial amount of it, particularly in the smaller towns of the South—it is pursued with varying degrees of enthusiasm. The diminishing national commitment to school integration is characteristic of a new phase in the continuing American dilemma of race and education: phase two, the second generation. The problems and issues now are infinitely more complex than they used to be, and they fall into one of two classifications. There is, first, the continuing problem of racial isolation, of segregation in the schools of the cities. Twenty years of litigating and demonstrating and procrastinating have made no appreciable dent at all in most big-city segregation patterns, and in spite of some continued talk about it, nobody seriously believes that segregation by race and economic class is going to be eliminated in such places as New York, Chicago, and Philadelphia—or Atlanta. Segregation in the big cities is a massive and immutable vestige of our racist past, and it is destined to be a part of the future. It was left completely untouched by first-generation desegregation, and except in a few big cities—again, mostly Southern—it is also unaffected by desegregation efforts in the second generation.

The other general category of racial issues in education revolves around those schools and school systems in which racial isolation has been overcome but second-generation problems predominate. After students have been reassigned and racially separate schools have been eliminated, a basic question remains: How do you create stable, equitable, racially and socioeconomically integrated schools that deliver high-quality comprehensive education to all children? The second generation of school desegregation—and all of the problems attendant to it—can be encircled by that one question.

Conditions and circumstances differ so greatly from state to state, city to city, school system to school system, that the notion of a national formula for equal educational opportunity now seems impossible, even ludicrous. There are no model solutions to the problem of racial isolation, or to the problem of inequity where isolation has been overcome. If there is a school system anywhere in the country that has fully resolved these problems, it has escaped the attention of legions of researchers. Life in American society is not molded by what goes on in the schools. The opposite is true: schools are a reflection of the values and priorities and prejudices of the larger society. The conflicts in American education today mirror the conflicts in the nation's cities and towns and rural communities.

So students and parents and educators and public officials and judges are still preoccupied, after two decades of controversy, with the manifold problems of inequality. What can be done in the schools about white flight and resegregation, about the long legacy of isolation and social incest, about the class struggle and the clash of cultures? What can be done about the inexperience and unpreparedness of adults to function effectively in a pluralistic society? How can democracy be made understandable or believable or workable in an educational system that is basically authoritarian? What can be done about the cumulative effects of discrimination and inequality? What can be done about a curriculum that was designed to prepare white children for life in a white society—and didn't even do that well? What can be done about children for whom violence is almost a way of life, for whom discipline and order and delayed gratification and material comfort are almost unknown? And what can be done about children who have known nothing but comfort and affluence and indulgence, all in isolation from anyone of a different race or class or culture? What can be done about ingrained, bone-deep white racism—the worse when it is unconscious and unintentional—and about seething black animosity toward whites? What can be done about teachers who teach subjects instead of children, and parents whose expectations are built around test scores and grades rather than knowledge and understanding? These are some of the questions that persist in the second generation of school desegregation. The search for answers is halting, glacial, erratic, and fraught with peril.

It is also unavoidable. More than a century of bitter experience has proved beyond any doubt the bankruptcy of racial isolation. There is nothing in the record of our history to justify a return to segregation, or to suggest that the nation's white majority would ever seriously attempt to make "separate but equal" work to the benefit of the nonwhite minority. School desegregation is no panacea for what ails us, but no realistic alternative exists if there is any hope at all of attaining even a semblance of equality in a society supposedly founded on that ideal. The Supreme Court put it succinctly in the *Brown* decision: "Separate educational facilities are inherently unequal."

But inherent inequality is a characteristic of American education, as it is of American society. Public schools are inadequately and inequitably funded, and the problem worsens steadily: school bond issues are voted down, school budget requests are continually reduced by local and state elected officials, and federal support of public education, after a decade of escalation, is now on the decline. The people who are charged with the educational process itself—the teachers, the bureaucrats, the college professors—show a general lack of skill and motivation to serve the needs of a diverse school population. The affluent minority—whites in the main, but not exclusively—are the only true possessors of freedom of choice: they can and do purchase educational alternatives for their children, and in the exercise of that choice they hasten the conversion of public education into what public housing has become—a place where minorities and the poor are confined against their will. And the gap between what is expected of schools and what they can deliver continues to widen. Regardless of what social scientists say about the effect of schooling, it is an article of faith among almost all Americans that education is the principal avenue to freedom and success and all the good things in life, and our multiple and conflicting perceptions of what "the good things" are can be seen in the diversity of offerings we expect and demand of our schools—college preparation, vocational and technical training, career education, religious indoctrination, athletic training, social and cultural refinement, patriotism, sex education, driver education, business education, and much more. And implicit in what we expect schools to do is a desire for the opposite of equality— for advantage and privilege and superiority, for a sort of chauvinism, whether based on race or sex or class or a particularized view of the American Way of Life. Nobody is fully exempt from that impulse: to make it, to get ahead, requires having somebody to get ahead of.

Under segregation, whites held a virtually complete advantage over blacks in the public schools. Beginning with the Supreme Court's decision in the *Brown* case, the federal government moved at a slow but steady pace toward the elimination of that advantage, and toward a consonance between the practices of the schools and the promises of the Constitution. The federal courts led that march, and they were eventually joined by the executive branch in the Kennedy and Johnson years, and by the Congress. President Nixon, though, has dramatically reversed that movement. Through his appointments to the Supreme Court, his instructions to education and justice department officials, his influence in Congress, and his promises to "the new American majority," he has brought about a retreat from integration in the schools and in the country at large. One of his domestic advisers in the White House, Patrick J. Buchanan, captured the essence of the Nixon attitude in a memo to the President in February 1972. Buchanan presented "a bill of particulars *against* any more compulsory integration, anywhere in the country at this point in time." He wrote in the memo: "The second era of Re-Construction is over; the ship of Integration is going down; it is not our ship; it belongs to national liberalism—and we cannot salvage it; and we ought not to be aboard." The memo could as easily have been written in 1968, for the President seems to have been guided by that philosophy since he first took office. Whether he was the principal creator of anti-integrationist sentiment in the country or the chief exploiter of a mood that already existed seems almost beside the point: the fact is that under his leadership the nation has adopted an attitude of resistance to equal educational opportunity that once was thought to be confined to the South.

The travail of public education, the spread of de facto segregation, and the national abandonment of the goal of integration are particularly ironic developments for many communities in the South. Having resisted integration by every means at their disposal, having endured the moral preachments of Northerners and submitted at last to the orders of the courts and the pressures of the executive branch, they find themselves now with desegregated school systems—just at a time when many Northerners and city dwellers and congressmen and liberals and social scientists and federal bureaucrats and even some judges are saying that "forced integration" is wrong and the elimination of segregation is impossible. One of the leading proponents of that view, Harvard University sociologist Nathan Glazer, told a Jackson, Mississippi, audience in the spring of 1973 that the Supreme Court should call a halt to the school integration process "for practical reasons," and he added: "I'm trying to find a moral justification for a line that cannot be neatly drawn by the courts." One of his listeners, a young Jacksonian deeply involved in that city's attempt to lift its school system out of the segregationist past, had this reaction to Glazer's comments: "I was brought up believing we were wrong in the South to practice segregation, and the North was somehow more enlightened, morally superior. Now we've changed—never mind *why* we changed, we did it—and we're trying to make it work. And just when we finally did it, the

North is showing us how hypocritical it is, and once again they seem to be looking down on us. It's as if they were laughing at us and saying, 'You suckers, you stupid jerks, you bought that integration line, and now you've got to live with it.' "

But the last laugh may yet belong to Southerners like him. It is possible to visualize a future time when the only school systems not incapacitated by the scourge of segregation and its manifold consequences will be those in Southern communities which moved under court pressure to erase the double standard based on race.

One such community is Greenville, South Carolina, which in February 1970 ended one day with a pattern of predominant segregation and began the next with a ratio of approximately eighty whites to twenty blacks in each of its ninety-one schools. Three years later, Greenville was still adjusting to its changed condition, but it was at least in a position to address itself to second-generation desegregation problems, and it had the prospect of an equitably integrated school system within its reach. Here is a glimpse at the Greenville schools in 1973:

About a quarter of a million people live in the 789-square-mile area encompassing Greenville and Greenville County, and they have been served by a single public school system for the past twenty years. Most of its 58,000 students were still in segregated schools at the beginning of 1970 when the Fourth U.S. Circuit Court of Appeals ended a long period of litigation with an order calling for immediate implementation of a racially balanced desegregation plan. (The order was signed by Chief Judge Clement F. Haynsworth, Jr., the man President Nixon nominated—and the Senate rejected—for a seat on the Supreme Court.)

Lacking any more viable options, Greenville proceeded to face the inevitable. The school board appointed a citizens' advisory committee to encourage peaceful compliance, the city's human relations committee and its chamber of commerce pitched in, the mayor and other public officials said their children would remain in the public schools, the governor promised obedience to the court ruling, the local newspapers editorialized about "the solemn duty of citizens" to obey the law, and before there was time for strong organized opposition to develop, the deed was done. The black community, in spite of some serious misgivings about inequities in the plan itself, was generally supportive of the end, if not the means.

An army of volunteers—some 2,000 in all—set up a telephone rumor-control center, distributed detailed information sheets published by the newspapers, worked with student government leaders and school officials, helped speed the buses on their new rounds, and generally aided in the transition. The plan required a 25 percent increase in the number of students riding buses, but it was handled with such finesse and it happened so quickly that people were surprised at the ease of it all. When an election was held soon afterward to replace the seventeen-member school board with a nine-member body, six members of the old board who stood for reelection were successful, and none of the three newcomers campaigned as opponents of the plan.

One of the carryover members was William N. Page, a bank executive who was credited with having led the board to devise the desegregation plan and close ranks behind it. He recalled later: "If we had had until September to make the change, we might have failed. People rallied to the challenge. There was a sort of hurricane atmosphere, and everything had to be done at once. After the board came around to the position that we would go the whole route, we never wavered. We had the business power structure and the religious establishment with us, and something very significant happened very rapidly."

That "very significant" happening lasted through the remainder of the school year, and the South Carolina educational television network recorded it in a film called "Integration with Grace and Style." Greenville seemed to be out of the woods.

The superintendent of the system retired that summer, and

Dr. J. Floyd Hall, his replacement, had been on the job only a few months when fighting between blacks and whites broke out in several high schools. Half a dozen private segregated schools had opened, enrollment in the public schools fell off by about 500, and black dissatisfaction with the plan boiled to the surface. The busing of a disproportionate percentage of black students, the closing of some black schools, and the displacement of some black administrators lay at the heart of those grievances, and Bill Page acknowledged the legitimacy of the complaints. "The way we did it involved the least amount of transportation and the maximum use of the best buildings in the system," he said. "It was the most logical way—which is not to say the fairest. It was mathematically correct, but it bothered me emotionally." It bothered the black community even more, and an effort was made to get relief from the court, but it failed. Superintendent Hall and the school system, caught between the erosion of black support and rising white segregationist fervor revived by President Nixon's antibusing stance, struggled through a period of conflict and uncertainty.

By the fall of 1972, there existed a generally widespread—if reluctant—acceptance of the new status quo. Leaders of the black community still sought more equitable treatment from school officials, and some organized white opposition to racial balance still existed, but in the main there was an atmosphere of calm in the schools. "The average man on the street without kids in school couldn't care less about all this," said Theo Mitchell, a black attorney, "but the people who are affected care very much. By almost any measurement you want to use, it is blacks who have had to pay the highest price for school desegregation as it's been done here. I'm not saying we shouldn't have done it—I'm no segregationist—but I am saying that it hasn't been done fairly." Ernest Harrill, a Furman University professor who headed the school system's first citizens' advisory committee, offered this characterization of white attitudes in the community: "People have changed some, in spite of themselves. The sky didn't fall in when we desegregated. But underground, the resistance is still there. It gets expressed as law and order, or antibusing, or declining discipline and morals, but it's all tied together. What progress we have made has been because of the force of law. Sad to say, we've been moved only by the law, and not by our own spirit."

Greenville's schools have desegregated, but they still have not integrated. The attitudes of many people remain unchanged, inherent discrepancies in the plan have not been fully corrected, the performance of teachers and administrators has improved but needs further strengthening, and the achievements of students in the classrooms still reflect the heritage of discrimination. The threat of further changes in federal policy that could irreparably damage the unitary school system hangs over Greenville like a storm cloud. The difficult job of equalizing opportunity without destroying diversity is still far from finished. The pace of change is too slow for some and too fast for others. Nevertheless, an overall impression of progress remains. Superintendent Hall, after three years on the job, says he is pleased with the general improvement of the schools, and he believes that both blacks and whites will become more and more supportive of them. More blacks will be elevated into the administrative ranks, he asserts, and new schools will be built near the heart of the city, closer to the black community. He expresses pride in the progress blacks have made academically, and he strongly disputes the claims of some whites that their academic progress has been adversely affected. "Within the next two or three years we're going to be in good shape," he said. "The right actions on our part will gain the confidence of the whole community."

The ultimate test of integration is inside the schools, among students and teachers and administrators. They are the ones who will show whether the best the school system has to offer is good enough—and what was happening in the Greenville schools after three and a half years of desegregation seemed to lend hope, if not substance, to Hall's optimism. To be sure, no state of perfection had been reached—there was still some friction and conflict. But the observation of a student at Wade Hampton High School seemed to represent something of a consensus. "The older integration gets, the better it gets," he said. "The ninth graders get along better than the seniors. The generation after ours is gonna have it all together. They may have a lot of other problems, but they're not gonna be hung up on the race thing."

For all the imperfections of desegregation in Greenville, and for all the external threats to its ultimate success, it has at least brought blacks and whites together in the schools, and it has given them an opportunity to begin their own search for an equitable educational and social contract. Segregation permitted no such possibility. The students seem less and less inclined to be influenced by the racial attitudes of their elders. As for the adults who are in a position to influence the character of the Greenville schools—the parents and teachers, administrators and board members, legislators and congressmen, judges and federal officials, and even the President of the United States—they may still decide whether integration and quality education there will be firmly established or finally destroyed. But they may also find that no matter what they do, the young people who are tomorrow's majority will be the ones who ultimately determine what Greenville does about race and education.

If Greenville is an example of a city trying to make school integration work, Atlanta looks more like one that has given up. There aren't very many cities similar to Greenville, in or out of the South, but the Atlanta pattern is all too familiar nationwide. "In a way," wrote Calvin Trillin in *The New Yorker*, "civic boosters [have] been correct in claiming that Atlanta [has] become a city of national rather than Southern stature: instead of businessmen talking about the dangers of becoming 'another Little Rock' or 'another New Orleans,' as they did in 1961, they were talking [in 1973] about the dangers of being 'another Newark.' "

Back in the early 1950s, the Atlanta public school system had 50,000 white students and 20,000 blacks. Ten years later there were 100,000 students, half of them white and half black. In 1973, white enrollment was down to about 20,000 and the black student population was approaching 80,000. Conventional wisdom has it that school desegregation frightens whites away, but Atlanta is proof that such a notion is too simplistic. Atlanta has never had much school desegregation—two-thirds of its schools are as segregated now as they ever were—but it has had massive white flight to the suburbs nonetheless, and its burgeoning black population now constitutes a majority in the city. The fear of impending desegregation no doubt accelerated the white exodus, but Atlanta's whites didn't try desegregation and then throw in the towel; most of them were already on their way to suburbia when the first blacks showed up. The result is that new phenomenon in American education: the predominantly black urban school system. Atlanta and New Orleans and Memphis and Richmond are following essentially the same public school trends and patterns as Cleveland, Detroit, Chicago, Philadelphia, Kansas City, St. Louis, Newark, Oakland, and Washington.

One telling commentary on the changing times is provided by Atlanta's two daily newspapers, the *Constitution* and the *Journal*. The legendary Ralph McGill single-handedly gave them an image of moderation and enlightenment back in the days of the civil rights movement; he was against segregation, and the papers more or less reflected that viewpoint. Now that the school integration issue has finally come home to Atlanta, the two papers have shown themselves to be not unlike "liberal" papers elsewhere: liberal with other people's problems at a distance, and reactionary with their own problems up close.

It is those up-close problems that have put white Americans,

North and South, in the same boat. School desegregation, virtually everywhere it has been tried, has placed the responsibility for change more heavily on blacks than on whites. It has usually been blacks whose schools were closed, whose principals were demoted, whose coaches and teachers were reassigned or released, and it has been black students who usually faced the greatest amount of busing. If all that disproportionate responsibility had been rewarded by the outcome, perhaps most blacks would have accepted it with equanimity. But the rewards have been few; most desegregation plans have perpetuated white advantage, and most have tended to reduce black identity and self-esteem, and most have failed to advance blacks to parity with whites in the educational process.

So now there are blacks who advocate separatism, or community control, or neighborhood schools. There are middle- and upper-class blacks who don't want their kids bused to school with the poor, whether black or white, and there are poor blacks who don't want their kids bused into hostile white suburban communities. There are, in short, a multiplicity of reasons why many black citizens are opposed to school integration as it has been pursued, just as there are many reasons why the opposition of whites to integration has remained strong, and perhaps even grown stronger, over the past twenty years.

In Atlanta, where blacks are the majority race, these diverse attitudes are strong and pervasive, and integrationists are scarce in both races. Whites, unable to visualize themselves as a minority, have tended to remain only in those schools where they outnumber blacks. And most blacks, seeing no particular attraction in that state of affairs, have gravitated—because they chose to, or because they had to—to the schools where whites are the least numerous.

In the spring of 1973 a group of influential blacks in Atlanta devised a compromise desegregation plan and presented it to the federal court. Under the plan, the city's twenty remaining all-white schools would each be assigned a black minority enrollment of about 30 percent, but the more than eighty all-black schools would be unaffected. There would be a bare minimum of busing, almost all of it by black children. At the same time, the retiring white superintendent would be replaced by a black, and over a period of time, half of the system's administrative positions would be filled by blacks. The school board and the local branch of the NAACP reached agreement on that compromise, but the national NAACP and the NAACP Legal Defense Fund, a separate organization long active in school litigation, raised vigorous objections to it, and Atlanta's black power structure was quickly divided fore and aft by the ensuing controversy. (Rightly or wrongly, the school plan invited comparison with another famous "Atlanta Compromise" in 1895, when Booker T. Washington addressed a conference of white devotees of Henry Grady's New South and voiced what was widely interpreted as acceptance of a subordinate role for Negroes.)

The district court bought the school compromise—and so, apparently, did the white power structure, which got in the black-initiated plan a better break for whites than could have been imagined under any other circumstances. The national NAACP, after suspending its Atlanta branch from membership, appealed the court ruling, and so did the Legal Defense Fund, which had its own alternate plan calling for complete desegregation—and thus a black majority—in every school. A third option, filed in court by the American Civil Liberties Union, proposed the merger of the Atlanta school system with predominantly white systems in surrounding counties, the result of which would be a 70 percent white system. Similar proposals affecting other cities around the country are already before the courts, and the first such case to be decided by the Supreme Court—a case involving Richmond, Virginia—resulted in a four-to-four deadlock. For the first time since *Brown*, the Supreme Court is split down the middle on the school desegregation question.

As the self-styled "city too busy to hate" and an oasis of racial moderation throughout the turbulent civil rights era, Atlanta has come to symbolize—as it did in Henry Grady's day—the leading edge of the newest "New South" movement. How it resolves its crisis of school segregation is of more than passing interest to other Southern cities, and indeed to cities all over the country. It can make all its schools majority-black through desegregation, it can make all of them majority-white through merger with other districts, or it can keep a few majority-white and a great many all-black by implementing the compromise—and whichever way it goes, it is sure to influence other communities as shackled by the albatross of racial inequality as it is.

Somewhere between Greenville and Atlanta, on the rocky road to racial equity, dozens of cities are grappling with second-generation desegregation problems and with the still-lingering dilemma of racial isolation. Further from success than Greenville, closer to it than Atlanta, they seem suspended in mid-passage, and in the national climate of disillusionment with the idea of integration, they are drifting. Nashville is a case in point.

If one were to sketch a profile of an urban community ideally suited to the achievement of school integration, Nashville would very nearly fit the picture. It has metropolitan government—a single political jurisdiction comprised of the city and surrounding Davidson County—and it has one public school system to serve the entire area. The total population of half a million is not so large as to be unmanageable, and its rate of growth is not precipitate. The black population, a stable 20 percent of the total, is not of sufficient proportion to make nervous whites fear the loss of their majority status, but it is large enough to command attention and respect. Most of the black population is concentrated near the geographical center of the district, and thus presents no insurmountable logistical problems in the development of school desegregation plans based on two-way busing. The city traditionally has been conservative and racist, but less rigidly so, perhaps, than many Deep South communities, and it seems to take pride in its manifestations of moderation and enlightenment and diversity. It has the supposedly liberalizing influence of a large academic community, at the center of which are four nationally prominent institutions—Vanderbilt and Fisk universities, Meharry Medical College, and George Peabody College for Teachers. It has a large middle- and upper-class population, including a substantial black middle class. It has the Nashville *Tennessean,* a Pulitzer Prize-winning newspaper with a progressive reputation; a diverse and thriving music industry that has thrust the city into the national entertainment spotlight; so many churches and national religious headquarters that it has been dubbed Vatican II; and some individual citizens well known nationally for their progressive contributions in the academic world, in politics and business, and in such organizations as the National League of Cities and the National Education Association.

With so many assets at its disposal, Nashville should be the envy of many an American city hopelessly locked into a seemingly irreversible pattern of segregation. It has had a priceless opportunity to lead the way out of that briar patch. But ever since an elementary school was dynamited after the first black children were enrolled in formerly all-white schools in 1957, Nashville has lacked the leadership, the courage, and the will to make equal educational opportunity a reality.

Nashville dallied with piecemeal desegregation for more than a decade before Avon Williams, a state senator and Legal Defense Fund attorney, took the school system back to court in 1969. Federal District Court Judge William E. Miller, who had ordered the first desegregation plan for Nashville in 1955, held in 1970 that the school system was still segregated, and he directed school officials to come up with a new plan.

In the ensuing year, there were these developments: The school board submitted a plan to the court that was acknowledged to be inadequate. Without ruling on the merits of the plan, Judge Miller granted a delay pending the outcome of a case before the Supreme Court that might clarify some ambiguous legal points. Judge Miller was elevated to the Sixth Circuit Court of Appeals, and a new district judge, L. Clure Morton, was assigned to the Nashville case. The school system hired a new director (superintendent), Dr. Elbert Brooks. The Supreme Court ruled in *Swann* v. *Mecklenburg* that buses are a legitimate tool in helping to overcome school segregation. Judge Morton held hearings on the Nashville case, and they were disrupted by a crowd of irate whites following the lead of an aspiring young politician named Casey Jenkins. Morton subsequently rejected both the school board plan and a proposal of the plaintiffs, and a team of experts from the Department of Health, Education, and Welfare was instructed to produce another alternative. The HEW team came up with a plan that left none of the system's 141 schools majority-black but allowed about 30 to remain virtually all-white. The plan was scrutinized and approved by two top Nixon administration officials—Attorney General John Mitchell and HEW Secretary Elliot Richardson—and Tennessee's Republican leaders— Governor Winfield Dunn and Senators Howard Baker and William Brock—were made aware of it and acquiesced in it. Casey Jenkins, in a political campaign against incumbent Mayor Beverly Briley, steered the city on a swing to the right, and in an air of antibusing hysteria, Briley managed to beat Jenkins in a runoff only by matching his opponent's rhetoric of defiance. And finally, the Nixon administration, after having prepared and approved the desegregation plan, made its full implementation all but impossible by refusing to permit the use of federal funds to buy the necessary additional buses.

When school opened in the fall of 1971, the bus fleet that had transported 34,000 children the previous year was put on staggered shifts to handle an additional 13,000. The Jenkins forces boycotted the schools for about two weeks, and by October, when the furor had subsided a bit, there were 88,500 students in school—7,000 fewer than the year before. Half a dozen new segregation academies were in operation, and all of the city's existing private schools experienced a surge in enrollment. A dozen public schools had a majority of black students as a result of the white flight, and the overall black enrollment increased three percentage points to 27 percent.

In the heat of the crisis, and in its aftermath, Nashville was virtually bereft of any constructive white leadership. With the Nixon administration by then running full tilt against school desegregation plans everywhere, with the public opinion polls showing enormous majorities opposed to busing, and with a presidential election year coming up, local officials and influential public citizens joined the clamor for some kind of drastic action to stop the buses. Mayor Briley hired private attorneys to take an admittedly fruitless appeal to the Supreme Court; Congressman Richard Fulton, a consistent voter for civil rights legislation in the past, saw his congressional seat threatened by Jenkins and came out strongly against busing; Senators Baker and Brock, denying that they had in any way been privy to the Nashville plan, urged Attorney General Mitchell and the Justice Department to join in the appeal against it; and even the *Tennessean*, when it mentioned the subject at all editorially, was vague and noncommittal. The school board, appointed to office by Briley, bowed meekly to the mayor's insistence on the appeal, although four of its nine members had the temerity to resist.

Nashville's black citizens were generally supportive of the desegregation plan, or at least reluctantly accepting of it, even though they bore a disproportionate share of the change. It was less-affected whites—and some who were not affected at all—who fought so hard to defeat it. At least three-fourths of the total population—and by some estimates, at least 90 percent of all whites—opposed busing for desegregation.

The school system, facing such massive community resistance—and having in its own ranks a large number of teachers and administrators who shared the attitudes of the resisters—staggered from crisis to crisis through the school year. After a summer respite, school opened in the fall of 1972 with another 3,000 fewer white students in attendance. (Between 1959 and 1972, while black enrollment was increasing by a few hundred, white enrollment declined by a total of 11,000.) A few more buses were available, thanks to an order from the court, but there was no discernible change in the attitude of the community, and the politicized busing issue was a national preoccupation. The Justice Department made an embarrassing attempt to repudiate the Nashville plan before the Sixth Circuit Court of Appeals, but its attorney was sternly lectured by the three-judge panel and sent packing back to Washington, and the futile appeal produced nothing—except a $50,000 fee for Mayor Briley's special attorneys, paid from the city treasury.

After the election, to no one's surprise, the clamor began to fade. Senator Baker and Congressman Fulton had stuck to their antibusing guns, and their more reactionary opponents were unable to tar them with a soft-on-busing brush; both incumbents won easy reelection. President Nixon rode back into the White House, Congress was in adjournment after spending weeks on the busing controversy, and back in Nashville, the only consolation for the beleaguered schools was that the second year of desegregation was quieter than the first. But government at every level—local, state, and federal—still refused to support the effort. Funds for buses and for badly needed new buildings were not available, resegregation continued in the wake of further white flight, and the school board and its staff seemed immobilized and stalemated.

When segregation was the order of the day in Nashville, black and poor children suffered most from the inadequacies of the educational program. By virtually every index—proficiency in mathematics, diversity of curriculum, strength of faculty, physical facilities, dropouts, suspensions—the schools of the black and the poor came out badly in comparison with the schools attended by affluent whites. Desegregation was a step in the direction of equalization, and if it had been extended to involve every school, it could have made possible a general improvement in the academic performance of black and poor children without any adverse effect on the performance of affluent whites.

As far as it went, the desegregation plan did have some positive effects. There was no reduction in the number of black teachers and administrators, most formerly all-black schools in the inner city were kept open and whites were bused in to them, and the faculties of every school in the system were racially balanced. But the plan didn't go far enough. Most of the approximately thirty schools that were unaffected by it—almost all of them in the outer reaches of suburbia—remained overwhelmingly white and affluent. White flight was greatest among students who were to have been bused to schools in the central city, and the result was that more than a dozen schools remained majority-black. Far too many teachers and administrators proved to be ill-suited for the changes they had to make, and many of them were not able to muster the skill, the enthusiasm, or the self-confidence to function effectively in a biracial setting. Finally, and perhaps most important, no effort at all was made to reduce socioeconomic as well as racial isolation: Roughly one-fifth of Nashville's public school children come from economically impoverished homes, but in more than fifty schools, one-third or more of the children were poor. Many schools identified as "integrated" were in fact schools where equal numbers of poor whites and poor blacks predominated. Almost invariably, the schools with the highest proportions of poor children exhibited the most severe problems of academic underachievement, discipline, absenteeism, and racial friction, whether they were majority-white or majority-black.

Two comparisons between the schools of the poor and the schools where enrollment remained predominantly white and affluent were especially revealing. First, a higher proportion of children in the affluent schools were being bused than in the poor schools—even though the greatest opposition to busing came from the white middle class. And second, the results of standardized tests showed that about 40 percent of all the children in the school system were seriously deficient in reading. In the schools of the affluent, the average number of children in that category was about 20 percent of the total enrollment; in the schools of the poor, the average was about 60 percent.

In order to achieve any appreciable reduction in these pervasive inequities, the school system would have to make major adjustments in the racial and socioeconomic distribution of its pupils, bolster and retrain its teaching and administrative staffs, and concentrate far more resources in the basic academic fields. But local support for public education in Nashville has suffered because the mayor and the Metropolitan Council don't like busing, state support has been reduced because white flight has lowered the enrollment, and federal support has been jeopardized because of policy changes in the Nixon administration. There will be no further desegregation until new buses can be bought, or new schools can be built, or housing patterns can be changed, or community attitudes can be modified—and there is no realistic prospect at all that any of those things is going to happen. After two years of partial desegregation, several members of the school board and the director of schools, Dr. Brooks, seemed in favor of a long-range plan to complete the job—something they had shown little enthusiasm for in the past—but the plan they were advocating would require the closing of schools in the inner city, the construction of new ones in the suburbs, and the "one-way" busing of inner-city children. If that would satisfy the mayor and the council, who control the purse strings, it probably would not satisfy the federal court, and it almost certainly would be unacceptable to the plaintiffs in the school case and to the black community in general.

So the Nashville school system is hanging on, somewhere

between its segregated past and a future condition that remains to be determined. It has less racial isolation and white flight and resegregation than many school districts, and more than some others; it is neither the best nor the worst of the South's—or the nation's—urban school systems. Even if they wanted to, the people who run the public schools in Nashville could not, by themselves, eliminate all of the remaining vestiges of racial and socioeconomic segregation and get on with the business of trying to develop a high-quality integrated school system. For that to happen, politicians and government leaders and citizens in general would have to want it, to demand it—and the spirit of segregation and elitism and economic privilege is still too prevalent to encourage much hope in such an eventuality.

In the nation, the court battles drag on, and de facto segregation continues to spread. There are experiments to give parents educational vouchers to buy school experiences for their children in the open market, and the old notion of federal aid to private schools has been resurrected. Alternative school ventures, in and out of the public sector, rise and fall like ducks in a shooting gallery, and schemes are being tested to let private enterprise operate public school systems under performance-guaranteed contracts. The elimination of compulsory attendance laws is being advocated (only Mississippi, poorest among the states in education, has stuck to that course), and some critics are seriously proposing that public schools simply be closed. Countless solutions to inequality are trotted out—compensatory education, equalized funding, community control, early childhood education, tracking and grouping by test scores, teacher retraining, changes in the home environment of children, redistribution of income. It is solemnly asserted by some that the poor will always be with us, and by others that intelligence is a result of heredity, not environment, hence schools are powerless to educate children. And while the arguments rage endlessly, a sobering reality remains: There are 46 million American children in the public schools, and the vast majority of them have no realistic alternative except to stay there and hope that the experience will somehow help to prepare them for adulthood. Good schools, even the best schools, could not single-handedly transform all of those children into free and equal and productive citizens; desegregated schools, even integrated schools, cannot fully erase the ill effects that centuries of segregation and discrimination have had, and continue to have, on Americans of every race. But the rationale for pursuing integrated schools is not that they can be a magic cure for all that ails us; it is rather that their opposite—schools organized and operated on the basis of racial and economic segregation—have been one of the monumental failures in our history as a democratic nation.

The early hope of many integrationists that an end to segregation would bring an end to discrimination and inequality has been dashed. Time and time again, in large and small school systems all over the country, desegregation has been followed by hostility and strife, by whites retreating in panic to private schools, by a steady diminution of blacks in teaching and administrative roles, by massive increases in suspensions and expulsions. It has exposed glaring deficiencies in the curriculum, widespread incompetence among educators, and alarming inadequacies in the academic achievement of children—inadequacies that apparently have not been lessened appreciably by the desegregation process. These discouraging developments have caused many people, blacks as well as whites, to abandon the pursuit of integration.

It would certainly be excessive to claim that school integration is working; the truth is that it has hardly been tried. But in some communities around the South, where desegregation has been mandated by the federal courts, thoroughgoing integration is at least a possibility, an attainable goal. In many of those places, discouragement is receding with the realization that progress is being made, and integration is being seen for the first time as a development that might, after all, serve the best interests of the whole community. There are people in those communities who no longer believe the rhetoric about the evils of busing. They reject the notion that school integration is a leveling process that robs the talented and homogenizes students into carbon copies of one another. They speak instead of a growing appreciation for diversity, and of the advantages to be gained from an understanding of different races and cultures.

Florida is one of the Southern states where school desegregation has made some impressive advances. Many of its counties, including some of the urban ones, have used busing to establish racial balance in the schools, and Governor Reubin Askew has set the tone for the changes that have taken place by openly and consistently supporting integration, not just in the schools but in public life generally. In 1972, when political campaigning was in full swing and busing was under heavy attack, Askew was pointedly reminding the people of the Northern states of their earlier self-righteousness:

For many years now, the rest of the nation has been saying to the South that it is morally wrong to deprive any citizen of an equal opportunity in life because of his color. I think most of us have come to agree with that. But now the time has come for the rest of the nation to live up to its own stated principles. Only now are the other regions themselves beginning to feel the effects of the movement to eliminate segregation.

I say that the rest of this nation should not abandon its principles when the going gets tough. I do not say this to be vindictive, I say it to be fair. The rest of the nation has sought to bring justice to the South by mandate and court order. Now perhaps it is time for the South to teach the same thing to other regions in a more effective way—by example. I certainly hope we will.

. . . I hope we can say to those who would keep us angry, confused and divided, that we are more concerned about justice than about transportation, and that while we are determined to solve both, we are going to have justice first.

When Oliver Brown went to court in Topeka twenty years ago, the conventional wisdom had it that school segregation was confined to the South and a few states on or near its borders. Now, segregation is acknowledged to exist all over the nation, and most of the notable exceptions to that pattern are in the South. Senators and congressmen from New York and Michigan and Ohio, in a bipartisan coalition with Southerners, are trying to pass an amendment to the U.S. Constitution that would prohibit busing—and threaten to re-create conditions that existed prior to 1954. And the governor of a Southern state has made an eloquent challenge to the North to "live up to its own stated principles."

Oliver Brown would no doubt be amazed. And saddened.

Industry: The New Carpetbaggers

"The South today means economic growth, a more highly skilled and unionized labor force, expanding cities and urban complexes, shifting political alliances, relatively stable race relations, a still pleasing environment, and rich new markets for all sorts of goods and services. . . . Like a developing country, the South has reached the 'takeoff' stage of its economic development."

So said *Business Week* magazine in a special report ("The Rich New South: Frontier for Growth") published in the fall of 1972. The report acknowledged some unaddressed and unresolved problems in the South—growing disparities in the distribution of wealth, increasing pollution and congestion and urban sprawl—but on the whole, it sketched a glowing profile: retail sales are rising at a faster rate than in the nation as a whole; unemployment is lower in the South; per capita income

104

is lower than the national average, but growing faster; land, labor, and raw materials are cheaper and more abundant; people are moving in faster than they are moving out. "New people bring fresh skills and bigger consumer markets," the report said. "New business diversifies and broadens the economic base, upgrades the labor force, raises wages, and creates new regional capital markets. Together, they spin off growing cities and suburbs, engender a strong middle class, shatter traditional social and political attitudes, homogenize the region, and build myriad bridges to the rest of the country."

Fortune magazine's annual listing of the nation's largest business enterprises verifies the march of prosperity to the South. Only half a dozen of the 100 largest industrial corporations on the 1972 list were Southern-based, but almost 90 percent of the top 500 corporations had regional operations in the South, and the South was headquarters for six of the fifty largest banks, eight of the fifty largest insurance companies, nine of the fifty biggest transportation companies, and fourteen of the fifty biggest utilities.

Industrial growth is setting new records in virtually every Southern state. Alabama, for example, reported more new and expanded industries, more new jobs, and more capital investment in 1972 than in any previous year in its history, and Governor George Wallace proclaimed that the state "has climbed back from the War Between the States" and rebuilt itself. He is only partly right: it *has* climbed back, but it has not rebuilt *itself*—Northern industrial and financial might and federal economic assistance have been the major factors in Alabama's move toward recovery and development.

The South's industry is constantly diversifying. It is not just food products, wood and paper products, textiles, and tobacco, as in the past, but also petrochemical products, electronics and aerospace facilities, and major financial institutions. And the region's airports, its seaports, its interstate highways, and its railroads are moving goods and supplies and people as never before. The Atlanta airport handled 20 million passengers in 1972—only the O'Hare airport in Chicago had more—and a new megaport serving Dallas and Fort Worth will be the largest in the world. All the coastal states from Florida to Texas have visions of developing a superport larger than any on the Gulf of Mexico, with inland waterways reaching as far as Dallas and north Alabama and Arkansas.

It is enough to make Marse Henry Grady, the nineteenth-century "New South" booster, rest contentedly in his grave. A burgeoning new middle class, laden with the largess of an affluent society, clogs the highways and airports, bound for weekends in the mountains, summers on the seashore, Saturdays and Sundays in the stadiums, semesters in Boston and Berkeley and Ann Arbor. Cars, boats, campers, cycles, electric appliances, stereos, and color television sets proliferate with rabbitlike rapidity. People are in a hurry, moving in, moving out, moving up; giant shopping malls and apartment complexes spring up like magic beanstalks, and fill up with people just as quickly; golf courses and country clubs and elegant resorts abound; Caribbean cruises and European vacations are commonplace; people indulge expensive and exotic tastes in food and clothes and liquor. The free-enterprise system, with a benevolent boost from government and the ironic stimulus of the war in Southeast Asia, has brought economic boom time to the American South, and almost everyone who is benefiting from it seems more preoccupied with the profits to be made than with the price to be paid.

Yet in the midst of all this growth and consumption, some troublesome questions intrude: What about all the people who are not sharing in the South's newfound affluence—who are, in fact, becoming further removed and separated from it? And what about the people who *are* getting theirs—what does the sudden availability of wealth and affluence do to people's values? And how can the growth and development and expansion of the South be controlled—how can the bulls be kept from stampeding?

Less than one-fourth of the people in the United States live in the South, but almost half of the nation's poor live there. No Southern state has a per capita income as high as the national average. The poorest 20 percent of the South's families receive less than 5 percent of the region's income, while the wealthiest one-fifth get almost 45 percent. The median family income for blacks in the South is only a little more than half as great as the median income for whites, and the actual dollar gap between white and black families increased by more than $350 during the 1960s. In the rural South, where more than 35 percent of the people still live, blacks and whites alike are plagued by poverty, unemployment, and underemployment— for the masses of them, work is scarce, pay is poor, and economic security is a day-to-day problem. Millions of Southerners are affected adversely, if at all, by the greening of Dixie.

Those who are benefiting—the entrepreneurs, the businessmen, the political and governmental leaders, the legions of salesmen and marketing experts and lenders and consultants and professional people, both Southerners and "outsiders"— are more or less characteristic of the people who profited when prosperity bloomed in the West, or when the North and the East were industrialized, or when the South went through Reconstruction and made its pitch for economic growth a century ago. The outsiders were called carpetbaggers then, and local beneficiaries were called scalawags. Then as now, they were a mixed bag—idealists and adventurers, visionaries and knaves, altruists and empire builders and avaricious con men. In almost no way does the industrialization of the South show concrete evidence of creative departures from the patterns of the past.

Former North Carolina Governor Terry Sanford, now the president of Duke University, has spearheaded the establishment of the Southern Growth Policies Board, a quasi-public agency which hopes to corral and contain the stampede of growth, and there is general acknowledgment that something needs to be done, but the march of industry proceeds apace, spreading its blessings and curses indiscriminately. People swarm into the cities, where the biggest new industries are concentrating, and the cities bulge and sag under the weight of the proliferating problems their growth causes: prices and taxes soar, values and mores collide, schools and housing become inadequate and overcrowded, streets and highways are clogged with traffic, crime and noise and pollution spread, public services break down, customs and cultures splinter, anonymity and impersonality take their toll, people have more and need more and want more—more money, more things, more time, more peace and quiet. And the beast of bigness goes on unchecked, spawning and devouring simultaneously.

The anti-industrialist Agrarians of half a century ago were wrong: their vision of "the good life"—a bucolic paradise uncontaminated by industrialization and its consequences—was a hopeless pipe dream, and would have resulted in the severest contrast between privilege and poverty even if it had been possible. Industrialization cannot be stopped; it is both inevitable and necessary. But Henry Grady and all the New South evangelists, past and present, are also wrong: the South cannot industrialize in uncritical emulation of the rest of the country without sacrificing its soul—and in its pell-mell rush to growth and development, it seems bent on duplicating every failure the Northern cities have experienced.

So a classic contradiction is created: the South cannot survive without industrialization—and may not survive with it.

Paradoxically, there are some small towns and rural areas where promising changes seem to be taking place. Here and there, school desegregation has produced surprising and encouraging results. In scattered locations, textile workers and migrant farm laborers and pulpwood workers are organizing across racial lines, forming unions to demand higher wages and better working conditions. The union movement, always weak in the South (only about 15 percent of all nonagricultural workers are unionized even now), seems certain to gain strength in rural areas as well as urban ones. Many poor people in sparsely populated sections of the South are forming cooperatives—farms, stores, small industries, child care centers, even schools—to gain some self-sufficiency and independence in the face of hostile circumstances. By the end of 1972, there were about 110 member organizations in the Federation of Southern Cooperatives, a coordinating body created to encourage the growth of collective enterprises among the poor, and to multiply their strength.

But these developments remain the exception rather than the rule. There are still company towns owned or dominated by the paper and timber and textile industries, and life in them is like a throwback to the past. White racism is still common and conspicuous in many parts of the South. Blacks have gained the power of the vote, and they have elected black mayors and sheriffs and judges and other public officials in some towns and counties, but whites still control the land and the wealth virtually everywhere. And in any event, the population is shifting rapidly to the urban centers—that is where the big industries are going, and that is where the Americanization of Dixie is in full flower.

Wherever new industry goes—whether to the largest metropolitan centers, the middle-size and smaller cities, or the little towns and county seats—it causes a variety of good and bad changes to take place. It changes the nature of work itself, it creates more and different job opportunities, it brings in new people with different ideas and life styles, it raises income, it affects race relations and education. In some places, corporate newcomers have taken their public responsibilities seriously, reasoning that it is in their own best interest to strengthen the social and cultural fabric of their adopted community. In others, the desire for quick profit above all else has been disastrous to the community. And always, the general public—the man in the street, the new employee, even the banker and the local establishment leader—see only the tip of the iceberg.

Sometimes the new carpetbaggers themselves cannot presage the consequences of their actions.

There is a small Southern city—call it Plainville—which made rapid strides from an agricultural to an industrial economy in the decade of the 1960s. Plainville is a city of 20,000 people—40 percent of them black—and the county in which it is located has about 70,000 people, more than half of whom are black. It used to be cotton and tobacco country, and it had all the familiar characteristics of the agricultural South—an unskilled work force, a low income level, a high degree of poverty, commonplace racial discrimination. There were a few small factories, but they didn't hire many workers, and they paid low wages, so most of the people either made their living off the land or made it from the people who worked the land.

Then the Northern corporations came, opening branch plants in the county, and by the middle of the decade they had hired 5,000 workers. Plainville welcomed them eagerly and generously, giving them free land and tax advantages and a labor force that could be employed cheaply. The state chipped in with a manpower training program, and both the corporations and the community thrived on the prosperity that ensued.

One of the first and largest of the companies to come to Plainville was a manufacturer of automotive parts, and its national sales manager happened to be a former classmate of mine, an old friend from twenty years past. I ran into him quite by accident in 1969, and he invited me to visit him in Plainville, and subsequently I did.

In order to tell the story I heard from my friend—about his adventures in the American marketplace, about the company he worked for, the people who ran it, the town they had come to—it is necessary to disguise real people and places with fictitious names. That is unfortunate; it protects the guilty as well as the innocent. But for reasons that will become obvious, that is the only way the story can be told. So we will call my friend Bill Robertson, and his employer the Victory Parts Company, and we will add more names later.

I remembered Bill Robertson from our school days as a friendly, humorous fellow, a good old boy from a small town in the Kentucky mountains. He is still a good old boy, in the best sense of that ambiguous Southern phrase, but the mark of the mountains has been polished away. He is no longer country, not even Southern; he is, instead, the quintessential American businessman—cool, precise, polished, fashionably dressed in an unostentatious way, soft-spoken and unexcitable, confident, impressive. He had changed tremendously, and I'm sure in his eyes he saw an equally vast change in me—we had grown from boyhood to manhood, and we were quite different men, different in outlook and interests—but we had been close friends, and as we retrieved memories from the past our reunion became a pleasant, satisfying thing, in a way that such experiences seldom do.

We went to dinner at his country club—Bill, his wife and I—and over a splendid cut of beef and a special bottle of wine we celebrated the good fortune of our chance meeting. Later, in the living room of their home, Bill and I talked on into the early morning hours, and it was then that he began to tell me, in his matter-of-fact way, a story that did not seem to fit with his steady eyes and casual smile.

He was troubled, frustrated. His company was making shoddy products of poor quality, and making them deliberately, and it fell his lot to sell those products, to misrepresent them to his customers. The reasons were complex, but the results were unmistakable: the next day, he took me on a tour of the plant, and in the stock rooms I saw row on row of parts ready for shipment. Even to my unpracticed eye, they were poorly made, flawed in numerous ways. "And not only am I selling junk to my customers," he said. "We have oversold it to the point where orders have piled up, and we can't even deliver what we're making, even though we promise prompt delivery."

I left Plainville that day, but the story Bill had begun to unfold stayed with me. A few months later, in 1970, we met in Memphis. His situation had worsened by then. I had my tape recorder along, and we had an evening to spend together, so I turned on the machine, and I asked him to go back to the beginning and tell me the whole story. He did, and here is the story Bill Robertson told:

I really started becoming disillusioned with the business world on my first job, right out of college. It was in the international division of one of the big automobile manufacturers. I spent a year here in this country as a trainee, and then a year in England, where I became a zone manager, calling on dealers. Then they sent me to the Middle East, to be a field parts manager. In those countries—Syria, Iraq, Iran, Jordan—restrictive money policies kept local people from taking money out of the country. There was not much way to do it, and the penalty if you did and got caught was death. So my company aided and abetted its auto dealers there, helped them cheat their governments out of money. The trick was false invoicing. In each country there was a central bank where the currency to buy foreign goods had to come from. A dealer in one of the countries would apply for, say, $200,000 to buy tractors. He would have a bill from the company that was actually 10 percent over the cost of the tractors—that was the understanding—and when the money was remitted back to the United States, back to the company, the dealer's 10 percent would be put into an account in his name at a New York bank. No one but the dealer, the bank, and a few officials of the company knew of it.

On one occasion, the commanding general of one of the country's armed forces wanted to buy about 2,500 trucks, and his "fee" for making sure our company got the order was $1 million. So we arranged with our dealer in that country to conceal the general's rakeoff in the invoice price of the trucks, along with the dealer's own percentage, and the deposits were subsequently made in their names in New York.

Once you get corruption at the top, it filters all the way down—everyone wants a rakeoff. It just happened that I was involved in some of those negotiations, I was in on them. Not many people in the company knew about them.

That experience really didn't disturb me, though—it wasn't all that disillusioning to me. Arabs are Arabs—you come to expect this sort of thing from them. So we just went along— they were so rotten that we couldn't have hurt them anyway, so we just went along with the game. But I never really thought about things of that nature happening in this country. Those were Arabs getting the rakeoffs, not Americans. The Americans did go away with lots of elaborate gifts, though—*baksheesh,* they called it: a tip, or bribe. My predecessor left with 25 watches worth up to $1,500 each. You don't accept a gift like that without the giver expecting something back from you. Nevertheless, I saw that as just one man's dishonesty, one American, so it didn't shake my confidence in any institutions. I had a very positive attitude about the free-enterprise system: In the free marketplace, shoddy goods would be driven out by superior goods, in the U.S. if not elsewhere. I believed that competition would take care of poor quality, and the system would take care of us.

I came back to the U.S. after two years and went to work for a management consulting firm in the Midwest, and by then I was very cognizant of the fact that there's a lot of dishonesty in the world. I really hadn't recognized it before, this possibility that corruption is everywhere, not just in a few isolated people and places.

I was in for a substantial shock, though, when I came back to this country and went to work with sixty bright young men in this consulting firm. Only two of us were not from the Ivy

League, and I was the only one without a graduate degree. We were supposedly the cream of the crop intellectually. I got the job because I had a Big Ten degree and had ranked second in my class, because I had some experience, and because I was lucky. This looked like a quick way to the top for me. I had (I'm not sure I still do) only one objective when I started out in business: to get to the top, be president of a company, make as much money as I could. I was very interested in power and money—they go hand in hand, of course—and I suppose, to be honest about it, I still am.

Anyway, the consulting firm experience was a real eye-opener. We double-billed clients routinely—you know, you make two stops on a trip, and you bill two different clients for the entire air fare. We were supposed to be the elite of the business, yet here we were involved in petty cheating. And we were dishonest in the reports we wrote, too. The Harvard boys had the writing skills, the verbal skills—even their thought processes were superior to mine. They knew more theory, they were more polished, they had that Eastern upbringing. I could write my reports in two to four paragraphs, but the clients expect forty to fifty pages, so that's what has to be done. Marketing problems are usually caused by individuals, not by products. But you couldn't tell a company's board, "Your vice-president for marketing is a jerk—fire him and your problem is solved." They wanted more, and all of it to serve, really, as justification for decisions they had already made.

I wanted out. I didn't like it for several reasons. I didn't like the basic dishonesty of it, and I didn't like working out solutions to marketing problems and then walking away and leaving implementation of changes to somebody else. So I took a job with an automotive equipment company. The automotive aftermarket—that's everything motor vehicles need after their initial sale—is one of the largest industries in the country, and I was interested in it as an area of specialization.

I was a regional sales manager for this company. I got no

reason to dislike the system from them—they weren't producing shoddy products deliberately—but they cheated their salesmen by juggling the books. I tried to let one guy get $600 he had coming to him, but they tricked him by inflating the value of the equipment he had charged out to him, and he got shafted out of his money. In his eyes, *I* had cheated him, and I didn't like having to be the bad guy.

In my three years there, that was the only thing that really upset me, as far as becoming disillusioned with people's honesty is concerned. But by 1968 I was ready to leave—I wasn't advancing, and I didn't want to get stuck there. So I started looking around, answering ads. I answered an ad in the *Wall Street Journal* for a national sales manager in a company selling car parts for the automotive aftermarket. This tool company, Victory Parts Company, had operated in a small city in the East for years and years. Back in the fifties it was bought by the Burton-Hunt Corporation, a big outfit that manufactured a whole range of automotive materials. Victory became the parts division of Burton-Hunt, and early in the sixties they moved it down to Plainville to take advantage of cheap labor and low taxes. Then Burton-Hunt bought out two more small companies in the North, and made them a part of the Victory operation in Plainville. All of this added up to only a small part of the Burton-Hunt enterprise. Everything they had in Plainville had been in trouble before they bought it, and Burton-Hunt didn't have the money or the technique to turn those companies around and make them profitable. They were reputable old firms with highly respected brand names, but they were old-fashioned, and they needed modernization. Burton-Hunt had moved them to Plainville and sort of forgotten about them, and when they took colored fellows out of the fields and put them to work on sophisticated equipment, quality and deliveries went to hell in a handbasket.

So in 1967, three young men in New York bought the entire Victory operation from Burton-Hunt, and it was a year after that when I saw their ad and answered it. These three guys were right around my age—thirty-five, give or take a couple of years—and they had all come out of the Graduate School of Business at Harvard. One of them was a marketing man, another was a manufacturing specialist, and the third was interested in acquisitions and finance. So they formed a partnership, and Meloy and Company, a big investment firm in New York, decided to sponsor them in a business venture—they had convinced Meloy that they had what it took to make it. One of the fellows set up an office at Meloy and spent a year and a half looking for suitable acquisitions. When they found Victory, they bought it for $10 million, using $2 million obtained from the sale of founders' stock—mostly to Meloy executives—and borrowing the other $8 million—again, with help from Meloy.

And that was the beginning of the ABC Corporation, which was from its inception a holding company. The three young men—Able, Baker, and Charlie—wanted to build a major conglomerate in the automotive aftermarket, and Victory was to be the centerpiece, the base.

Able and Baker moved to Plainville and took over, leaving Charlie in New York to look for more acquisitions.

Burton-Hunt had made a calculated risk in moving to Plainville. They had low wage rates, no union, tax incentives from the community and the state, but they had to contend with an unskilled labor force. They had some training costs and a high scrappage rate, but they still stood to make a hell of a lot bigger profit. They imported all their employees except the laborers, and they paid less than half what it would have cost them elsewhere for their assembly-line workers and even for the skilled people, like the tool and die makers.

But Victory Parts didn't even have a sales force. They depended on customers to come to them with orders. They were trading on the reputation of their old-line tools. They had absentee management—even the general manager and the sales manager didn't live in Plainville. The ABC men changed all that. They didn't pay people any more, or use any more local people, but they assumed personal control of the operation. They had one thing in mind: to build a conglomerate. They were sophisticated in the techniques of buying companies, inflating such things as good will, profits and income, and hiding costs. They were out to make a killing.

After they bought Victory, they picked up a couple of companies in the Midwest, and then another one in the East—all of them in the auto aftermarket. They used shares of their own stock to make these purchases. It was like a chain letter: the first guys in always clean up. By pooling these companies together in the ABC Corporation, they were able to give a totally inaccurate picture of the corporation to the public, and even to the prospective purchaser of stocks. Those who bought founders' stock, of course, were actually a part of the original scheme, and they were in on the initial kill. That goes back to Meloy—they understood, they calculated, and they cleaned up. By inflating profits on paper, by inflating sales and concealing costs, your financial reports are glowing, and that draws in new investors and lets you make more stock offerings, and the price of your stock keeps on rising. The people who bought founders' stock in ABC—the three partners, people at Meloy, and a few others—got it for ten cents a share. When the price got up to six dollars, the Meloy people sold most of theirs and got out.

In our economic situation in the mid-sixties, conglomerates flowered. But they can only thrive as long as the market is going up and business is good. In the turndown, they fell first because everyone knew there was probably something phony about their accounting methods. In other words, nobody cared very much as long as they were making money—it was only when they started losing that people got concerned.

Anyway, they did all this the first year, and they made ABC look like a beautiful cherry just begging to be picked. Acquisitions were made to look like internally built sales, like real growth. Burton-Hunt had been losing money because of poor quality, poor delivery, and a lot of scrappage. Their calculated risk had failed, and they weren't devoting the time and effort to make it go, and that losing record was precisely what made Victory so attractive to ABC: they had these three old-line companies, with names recognized and respected in the industry, and they had fallen on hard times. The three partners really thought they could make it go, and the paper earnings were going to be just icing on the cake.

They bought more—a wrench company out West, a company that sold tool kits to the military—and Victory was the base, the pillar. In the five years before Burton-Hunt sold Victory to ABC, it lost $4 million. In the first year after the sale, the loss was $750,000. In 1968 we *made* $750,000, and last year we made $1.8 million. But the ABC Corporation only made $920,000, so that means the other companies in the conglomerate weren't carrying their share of the load. In other words, as the sales manager for Victory Parts, I brought in $1.8 million, while everybody else was losing like hell.

But I'm getting ahead of the story. Near the end of 1967, when I answered the *Wall Street Journal* ad, Jack Able, one of the three partners, came to see me and interviewed me for the sales manager job at Victory. He was an impressive man, a management consultant expert, and he had big plans and made them sound exciting. He and Joe Baker were already living in Plainville, and Charlie, the third partner, was in New York. I was still a believer then. I had seen a lot to disturb me, but not enough to shake my faith in the free-enterprise system. And here was a man who wanted to make the best damn tools in the marketplace, and he was asking me to join them. It was a hell of a challenge. I scouted it out very carefully, visited their distributors and all, and I saw it as my big chance, so I took the job, and in January of 1968, we moved to Plainville.

Meloy and Company was still involved then, of course, and

they have only one objective in life: to turn a profit, the bigger
the better. Not provide jobs, not make better tools, not meet a
social obligation, just turn a profit, make a pile. My motives
were different: I wanted to make the best tools on the market,
and have satisfied customers, and make good money. Like I've
said, I wanted power and money, I wanted to do something
good, to feel like I had contributed something to society. If I
could do something good in life, and people would pay me
good money for doing it, that's what I'd like to do.

Technically, I work for Victory, but in fact I'm like the vice-
president for sales and marketing for the ABC Corporation.
I'm in charge of marketing for the entire conglomerate, but
things become very ill-defined and there's no way to draw a
formal organization chart. They offered me a big salary increase to take the job, but it was stock options that really got
me. I got 5,000 shares, which at that time were worth $12 a
share, and we truly felt we could take the price to $100 within
three years. Our timetable for making a public sale of stock
had to be changed when we bought a company that was already selling its stock over the counter at four dollars a share,
so ABC became a public company held by its founders and by
the stockholders of the company we had bought. The stock shot
up to eighteen dollars a share after we acquired the company.
We calculated its real value to be twelve. We wanted to register
on the American Stock Exchange, but we never made it, even
though we did get clearance from the Securities and Exchange
Commission to register 4 million shares for sale whenever we
were ready. And each of the three original partners had
$15,900 invested in the entire enterprise; they each owned
159,000 shares of stock which they had bought at ten cents a
share.

By the middle of 1969, trouble was brewing. The market
was declining, we had a large debt payment coming due, and
there was no way on earth to keep from selling stock to pay the
debt. So we had to go out in a depressed market and sell a big

batch of shares at four, even though we were sure they were worth twelve. About that time, Jack Able sold out and left to take a post in the federal government.

We had other problems, too. When I first went with the company, we exerted a lot of effort and made a lot of promises. A big inventory had been built up because under Burton-Hunt they had lost a lot of customers. We started moving it out; we promised 100 percent delivery in fifteen days, and we meant it. I fired a bunch of people and hired new ones, and I drove the hell out of them. I knew the marketplace, knew where to find the men I wanted. We were all fired up, and we were adding customers by the dozen, and we soared. I knew the sales potential better than the owners, and when sales increased by 40 percent very quickly, they were bug-eyed.

Baker, the manufacturing specialist, was the one who caused our real problem. His greed blinded him. He thought that just because we had had a big inventory before we boosted sales, we would be able to keep it. But by August, there were no parts—we didn't have a part in the house. We were badly over-sold, and our deliveries fell like a stone. So Baker says, "No sweat. We'll catch up." And how? He figured it out real fast: You cut quality, cut steps out of the routings, skip some of the stations in the manufacturing process.

At that time, we were making approximately 2,000 different parts, and there are, on the average, about twenty steps in the making of a part. That's 40,000 operations to make our product. Within a few months, we cut out at least 2,000 operations—5 percent of the total manufacturing process. You stop making a counter sink, you stop putting a hole in the handle, you stop holding it on the polishing belt so long, you reduce the polish under the chrome—I could go on and on. It was Baker's decision; Able was deceived because he didn't know the manufacturing process, and he was getting ready to leave anyway. So we got the parts out faster, and because they were selling so well, we were making more money on them by

cutting the cost. Kill two birds with one stone. It was a deliberately planned thing. And I had to sell the damn things for
them. And with people producing more parts per hour, we had
to cut back the bonus system because we were paying them too
much. They weren't aware of what was going on, not even the
foremen, because they see such a small part of the process.

Able really left because he wanted us to develop new programs and go after new markets, and Baker wanted to cut back
more, cut out some of the kinds and brands of parts we were
making. That way, he thought, he could make parts as fast as
we could sell them. He didn't understand that I was out there
fighting competition, and I needed the full line of parts—top-
quality parts—to be competitive.

So Able left, and now Baker is in total control. He's closing
out all but one line. I say, "We've got customers who have been
buying these old-line parts for a hundred years." He says,
"Screw them. They won't leave us. They owe us too much." So
we're consolidating the line. I'm out selling customers something I know they're not going to get. I'm lying to them, de-
ceiving them. They'll send the parts back to us, but Baker says,
"That's tomorrow. We'll worry about it then."

Now we're in a bad market. The stock is down to two. The
man who owned that company we bought when we went public
thought he was sure of making at least $3 million. Now he's
got stocks that are worth about one-fifth that much. He's
headed for a total wipeout of a lifetime's work—and not because of a market condition or an economic downturn, but
because he got hooked up with someone who thought you
could sell lesser quality and make a higher gross margin
and do anything on earth you want to a customer and still keep
him. And there just ain't no way to do it. And Baker is forced
to do it, because he's got Meloy and Company breathing down
his neck. They're only interested in money, and they're telling
him, "Friend, you turn it in to us or your ass is fried." What
looked like benevolence on their part was simply greed.

They're going to be left with a bomb-out, but they've already made a fantastic profit, and there's no way for them to lose.

The dream of turning Victory Parts and the ABC Corporation into an attractive buy for a bigger conglomerate—the dream of making a real killing—is dead. We're losing the customers we worked so hard—and in good faith—to win. And my salesmen are saying, "Bill, you lied to us, you told us everything imaginable, and lived up to none of it."

The stock options I got were not exercisable for two years, and after that, I was supposed to have three years to buy any or all of them at the price agreed to when I got the options. Altogether, I've got 10,000 shares available to me at an average value of eight and a quarter. I thought it was going up to sixty or a hundred, but it's selling now for two.

The consequences of all this for Plainville are almost catastrophic. The biggest plant there has already closed, taking $600,000 a month out of the local economy. Their home office is discontinuing the line of machines they made there, so they just shut down. If we close in a few months, we'll wipe out an annual payroll of $3 million and put another 650 people out of work. Baker would say, "It doesn't matter. They were nothing when we got there, and they won't be anything when we leave." But they'll be in worse shape than before, because they have briefly enjoyed a better standard of living.

If I've done nothing more than convey to you that our business is rotten to the core through greed, then I've succeeded, because I honestly believe that now. I realize now that this is really the way business is. That's the reason I'm disturbed. Look at your TV set, your car, your clothes. Everything's the same crummy quality, and I'm part and parcel of this, and I don't like it. My company is the leader of the shoddiness—I just happen to be associated with one that's one of the worst. Somehow I attribute our troubles to affluence; morals go. Dress. Movies. Literature. Cars. Sex. Everything can be had. Everybody's dishonest, everybody's trying to get his. The bloody government is the only one who can step in and protect you and me, and they're more dishonest than the guys in business.

So who's going to protect us? Do we need consumer legislation to protect people from people like me? Do you want to be protected from the Bill Robertsons of the world? It just isn't going to work. There's going to be a total collapse somewhere down the line. Consumer protection would be the answer if you could have any faith in the government, but you can't. We're almost a lost cause. I don't know where we go. Not socialism or communism—that's government control. Maybe we'll have to do like the college kids are doing: explode the whole bleeding system. Maybe we should start all over from scratch with barter deals, or something like that. I just don't know. But I do know one thing: You can't live through experiences like the ones I've had and still feel good about the free-enterprise system, or about your country, or about yourself.

Not long after he told me that story, Bill Robertson walked away from his worthless stock options, from Joe Baker and the whole mess, and went somewhere else to work. The ABC Corporation and Victory Parts Company are still hanging on in Plainville. Of the three original partners, only Charlie, the man in New York, has any continuing involvement. Baker got out in 1971, and the owner of the company they bought when they went public—the man who thought he had $3 million in the bag—is now in command.

When Victory first moved to Plainville more than ten years ago, back when it was owned by Burton-Hunt, it got a free plant site, free installation of sewers and utilities, a discount on utility rates, freedom from property taxes for five years, and a free employee training program set up by the state. In return, the company put 800 people to work—85 percent of them men—and paid them the minimum wage. About 400 people are employed there now, and the minimum wage still prevails.

If it had not attracted Victory Parts and the other factories, Plainville might have withered up and died. Instead, it survived the transition from an agricultural to an industrial economy, and it enjoyed a decade of relative prosperity—and it also survived, coincidentally, another transformation: from harsh and unbending racial segregation to the beginning of desegregation. But now its biggest industry is gone, and its second biggest—Victory—hangs precariously on the edge of failure. Plainville could still wither up and die.

But it probably won't. Other corporations are being courted. The state, like all Southern states, is searching for new capital to keep the wheels of progress rolling. The national economy is still not healthy, but it is not in recession anymore, and corporations are beginning to look again for favorable locations in which to expand. The South is the new industrial frontier, and Plainville shows why: the cheap and abundant labor force is still there, and the unions are still weak, and the weather is still good. If Victory dies, Plainville will go on living, and somebody else with an eye for profit will come along to nourish the people's newfound appetite for prosperity, to help them in their search for the good life.

In the march of American industry, the ABC Corporation is a small-change operation, and its manipulations in Plainville have been neither extensive enough nor corrupt enough to warrant more than passing notice in an age of commonplace dishonesty. With military contractors making millions of dollars on cost overruns, with multinational corporations attempting to influence elections not only in the United States but in foreign countries, with companies cheating their competitors as well as their customers, with wealthy Americans routinely escaping payment of their income taxes, and with public officials in the Justice Department and the White House itself giving law and order a bad name, nobody pays much attention to minor-league rip-offs such as the one in Plainville—and nobody knows how many Plainvilles there are. Surely there are some honest businessmen left; only the most hardened cynic could believe otherwise. But corporate criminality—what Ralph Nader has called crime in the suites—seems almost as common as crime in the streets.

Under the circumstances, Plainville has been fortunate: Victory Parts was not all the community had, and the company was not big enough or exploitative enough to cause the kind of grief and destruction that some industries produce. Victory did not precipitate massive depersonalization and monotony on the assembly line, it did not destroy natural resources or force families off their land or pollute the air or poison the streams. It created no local millionaires, and no local paupers. All it did was give a few avaricious men a springboard to personal wealth, and nudge a small Southern city closer to the currents and undertows of the American economic mainstream. In the tradition of American free enterprise, Victory is what it's all about.

Politics: A Southern Strategy from Coast to Coast?

On the 12th of October, 1972, Richard Milhous Nixon captured Atlanta. A sea of humanity—by most estimates, more than half a million people—parted along Peachtree Street to make way for the presidential motorcade, and a beaming President, his upraised arms and fingers telegraphing V-for-Victory signs, rode in an open limousine through a blizzard of confetti as the cheers of the throng reverberated about him and echoed up and down the concrete canyon.

His triumphant entry into the unofficial capital of the American South must have given Mr. Nixon a singular and unforgettable sense of satisfaction. Exactly 108 years before, the city was occupied by the Union army troops of General William Tecumseh Sherman, and in all the intervening years, no Yankee Republican—not even Dwight David Eisenhower—had been so warmly received there. Now he, Richard Nixon, had taken Atlanta without lighting a torch or firing a shot, and it belonged to him more completely than it ever belonged to Sherman or his commander in chief, a Yankee Republican named Abraham Lincoln. More than that, the region that once was known as the Solid South—solid for Democrats, solid against anyone wearing Lincoln's political label—was now about to become solid once again, this time for Nixon and the Grand Old Party.

The election came three weeks after that visit, but it was by then a mere formality. Nobody, with the possible exception of his Democratic opponent, Senator George McGovern, seriously doubted that Nixon would sweep to victory. In a landslide of gigantic proportions, he captured forty-nine of the fifty states, and the South led the way, giving him majorities of three-to-one and better. The trip to Atlanta—his first and only campaign foray into the South—turned out to be a pleasant but unnecessary political exercise.

At a high-level gathering of Southern Republicans that day, Nixon took the occasion to say how instrumental the South was in his "game plan" for reelection. The region, he suggested, was not really any different from the rest of the country; people everywhere were concerned about the same things, and he had addressed himself to those concerns—to military strength, peace with honor in Southeast Asia, national prosperity, law and order with justice, national growth and progress, patriotism, the strengthening of moral values. These are the "number one issues," he said, "the number one issues in the South and the number one issues in the nation . . . the issues that make most Southerners potential members of what we call the new American majority."

The President told his audience: "It has been suggested that by campaigning in the South in 1960, and then again in 1968, and now again in 1972, means that we have, I have, a so-called Southern strategy. It is not a Southern strategy; it is an American strategy. That is what it is and that is what the

South believes in and that is what America believes in. . . . There was a time in the South when any Southerner would vote for any Democrat and never vote for a Republican . . . that is no longer going to be true."

As if to underscore the key element in his capture of the South, Nixon brought up the subject of race early in his remarks. Race was the issue that had kept the South in the Democratic party and out of the national political mainstream; now, he intimated, it was one of the principal issues unifying his "new American majority." He spoke to the Republicans about it in these words:

> Now let me come right down to the issues. What are the so-called southern issues? This answer is going to surprise you. They are the same here as they are in America. Let me take the one that everybody assumes is a southern issue. I say everybody. Everybody who takes a superficial view of politics and thinks of the old politics and the old South, rather than the new politics and the new South, it is said that the major issue in the South is race.
>
> Let me tell you something. I was looking at some polls recently. I know, too, that the issue of busing is one that is a very hot one right here in this state. But as I was looking at some polls of various issues in the state of Michigan, and in the state of Alabama, did you know that busing is a much hotter issue in Michigan today than it is in Alabama?
>
> Now, what does that mean? It does not mean that the majority of people in Michigan are racists any more than the majority of the people of Alabama because they happen to be opposed to busing. It simply means this: it means parents in Michigan, like parents in Alabama and parents in Georgia and parents all over the country, want better education for their children, and that better education is going to come in schools that are closer to home and not clear across town.
>
> That is why our approach is better education, better education for all and equal opportunity for all, but not inviting into this particular matter the kind of approach that might, in the name of so-called racial balance, produce inferior education and racial strife.

We need better education for white children, for black children, and for all children. The way we can get it is, I think, through the approach I have suggested.

Now, getting that issue out of the way, let me tell you. . . .

And so much for that. His handling of racial issues, probably more than any others, explains how Nixon has succeeded in capturing from the Democratic party the support of a large majority of white voters in the South. In 1968, when he squeezed past Hubert Humphrey into the White House, he got 36 percent of the vote in the eleven Southern states; Alabama Governor George C. Wallace got 33 percent, and Humphrey finished third with 31 percent. Nixon's Southern strategy was fashioned in the heat of that campaign. Recognizing the seriousness of Wallace's threat, he unabashedly appropriated some of the Alabama governor's principal weapons of attack: he came out against busing as a means of achieving school desegregation, he promised to appoint "strict constructionists" who shared his judicial philosophy to the Supreme Court, he took a tough stance on "law and order," and he wooed and won some of the South's most conservative politicians, chief among them being South Carolina Senator Strom Thurmond.

It took all of that for him to come out a winner. During his first term the strategy was further refined, but in the 1972 primaries, George Wallace showed even more strength than he had in the past, winning over Democratic opponents not only in the South but in such pivotal Northern states as Michigan. In the sophisticated code language of the seventies, the man who once pledged, after a political defeat, never to be "outniggered" again, was keeping his pledge with a vengeance, and most of his opponents, Democrats as well as Mr. Nixon, were being drawn steadily to the right.

In the midst of all the maneuvering, Wallace was gunned down with a cheap revolver by the crew-cut son of a Michigan workingman—yet another incredible irony in what has become the surrealistic world of American politics—and by the time Nixon got to Atlanta, the only man who posed a serious threat to his Southern strategy and his new American majority was paralyzed and out of the race. Further, the President by then had been to Peking and Moscow, and he was promising an imminent end to the war in Vietnam, and the Democrats were coming apart over the nomination of George McGovern, a man Nixon's strategists gleefully labeled a radical advocate of "amnesty, acid, and abortion." All the breaks were falling the President's way; he was a sure bet for reelection.

The majority he won at the polls, in the South especially, turned out to be almost the exact sum of the Nixon and Wallace totals in 1968. In the South, McGovern got Humphrey's 30 percent; Nixon got the 70 percent he and Wallace had shared. Harry Dent, the South Carolinian who as a Nixon aide had helped to design the Southern strategy, said after the election that the South was once again a one-party region— this time for the GOP—and he added: "The South will never go back . . . the Republican beachhead is so well established. People in the South now realize that they have been Republicans philosophically for a long time."

Nixon's own understanding of that philosophical affinity probably comes closest to explaining how he has become a two-term president after losing one race for that office and subsequently suffering an embarrassing defeat in a campaign for the governorship of California. In his first try for the presidency, Nixon experienced limited success in cracking the Solid South, as did Eisenhower twice before him. Barry Goldwater in 1964 carried five Deep South states, but he was humiliated nationally by Lyndon Johnson, a Southerner who, in another of those classic ironies, left office four years later having done more to end segregation and white supremacy than any other President in history. But when he got a second chance, and after that a third one, Nixon succeeded where Goldwater failed: he Americanized the politics of Dixie and managed to hold his own in the rest of the country, and in 1972 he swept to an easy victory behind a national force of mostly white, mostly

middle- and upper-class voters who vastly outnumbered the
poor, the racial minorities, and the white liberals.

To be sure, the Americanization of Southern politics is a
more complex and ambiguous development than the election
and reelection of Richard Nixon alone suggests, just as there is
more to the Southernization of American politics than the rise
of George Wallace can explain by itself. The one represents a
bringing of the South into the midst of national trends and
movements; the other is a national acceptance of things Southern in origin; and in both of these developments, other influences are being felt besides those generated by Nixon and
Wallace.

Over and above Nixon's successes, the end of one-party
politics in the South is surely a positive and hopeful sign. The
region's twenty-two U.S. senators now include fourteen Democrats, seven Republicans and one Independent Democrat.
Among its 108 congressmen are seventy-four Democrats and
thirty-four Republicans, and each of the eleven states has at
least one Republican representative. Three of the states now
have Republican governors. State legislatures and local governments at all levels also reflect this trend, although grass-roots
Republicanism is still not broadly established. Numan V.
Bartley and Hugh Davis Graham, in a study of Southern politics from 1948 to 1972, note that the existence of three substantial and relatively distinct voting groups—blacks, low-
income whites, and the urban bourgeoisie—have "given rise to
a new—or at least different—politics in the South." It would
be easy to attach too much importance to this change, and
Bartley and Graham wisely refrain from doing so. "Much of
the turbulence of recent Southern politics has resulted," they
assert, "from attempts to force these three groups into the
normal mold of two-party competition." The turbulence remains as new factions emerge and splinter—there are old-line
conservative Democrats, New Deal liberals, old-guard Republicans, progressive urban Republicans, populist Democrats,

Wallaceites, women and youth groups that very nearly constitute independent forces, black Democrats, black third-party groups, and even blacks for Nixon. All that is reflective of national trends, and it is fractious and confusing, but in the South, at least, it is certainly more to be desired than the monolithic rigidity of one-party rule.

Still, if there was any thought that this opening up of the political process would immediately usher in an age of enlightenment and responsibility, that hope was premature, if not completely misplaced. Reapportionment, the two-party system, and the addition of urban dwellers, women, blacks, and young people may have begun to alter the image of state legislatures as clubs for middle-aged and elderly white males from the country, but those changes have not ended the conflicts of interest, the catering to lobbyists, the junketeering, the self-serving indulgences, the buffoonery, the time-wasting, the money-wasting, or the irresponsible lawmaking that are the sad mark of so many legislatures.

Reforms in the national Democratic party since 1968 have substantially increased the participation of women, minority groups, and young people and diluted the influence and control of old-guard white males, and the South has accepted those reforms as conscientiously as any other region—and more readily than most. A related development—the formation of the National Women's Political Caucus—also has attracted strong Southern participation. The national chairman of the caucus is Frances Farenthold, a reform-minded Texas Democrat, who was elected to the post at a February 1973 convention; she beat another Southerner, Martha McKay of North Carolina. The caucus is organized in all fifty states and has more than 30,000 members. Farenthold, a lawyer and former legislator, finished second in a field of seven in the race for governor of Texas in 1972, and she was nominated for vice-president—and finished second—at the Democratic National Convention the same year. Another Texas woman, Barbara

Jordan of Houston, was elected to Congress in 1972, becoming the first black and the first woman to join that state's delegation in the House of Representatives in modern times. She also became the only woman among the 130 Southern members of the House and Senate (Lindy Boggs, the widow of Louisiana Congressman Hale Boggs, soon joined her), and that fact shows that Southern women, like Southern blacks, are still vastly underrepresented in the national political picture.

There were thirteen black congressmen and one black senator in Washington before Jordan and Andrew Young of Atlanta and Yvonne B. Burke of Los Angeles were elected in 1972, but the growth of black voting strength in the South and the increase in black elected officials there have been so pronounced in recent years that the phenomenon can fairly be said to have influenced the national political process as much as that process has influenced the South. Black political power, in other words, seems a better example of the Southernization of American politics than of the Americanization of Southern politics. While it has been exporting the philosophy of George Wallace, the South has also been sending abroad the example of across-the-board black participation in political activity.

Before turning to Wallace and black political power, however, something more should be said about the Americanizing process in Southern politics. In spite of the gains it has made in abandoning one-party rule, and regardless of its receptivity to the political participation of blacks, youth, and women, the South's political behavior has been nationalized more by Richard Nixon's influence than by any other factor, and that is, for the South, a tragic misfortune. At a time of such crucial importance in its history, when it seemed so close to escaping from 350 years of imprisonment in the master-slave mentality— whites over blacks, North over South, rich over poor—the replacement of Lyndon Johnson with Richard Nixon was a devastating blow.

A bit of historical perspective is helpful to an understanding of just how much the South gained under Johnson, and how much it is losing under Nixon. In March of 1956, nineteen of the South's twenty-two senators and eighty-one of its 106 congressmen signed an infamous document that came to be known as the Southern Manifesto. Officially labeled a "Declaration of Constitutional Principles," it was an attack on the U.S. Supreme Court's 1954 decision outlawing racial segregation in public education. It called the court's decision an exercise of "naked judicial power" and a "clear abuse of judicial power." It asserted that the "separate but equal" doctrine under which segregation was practiced was "a part of the life of the people of many of the states," that it "confirmed their habits, customs, traditions and way of life," and that it was "founded on elemental humanity and common sense." The members of the court, the manifesto said, had "substituted their personal and political and social ideas for the established law of the land." The document condemned "encroachments on rights reserved to the states," it commended "the motives of those states which have declared the intention to resist forced integration by any lawful means," it pledged the signers "to use all lawful means to bring about a reversal of this decision," and it appealed "to our people not to be provoked by the agitators and troublemakers invading our states and to scrupulously refrain from disorder and lawless acts."

Coming as it did almost two years after the court decision, the manifesto was not the impetuous reaction of a shocked South but a calculated declaration of defiance by one hundred men in the houses of national political power. After it had been solemnly read on the floor of the Senate by Senator Walter George of Georgia, Senator Pat McNamara of Michigan declared that "no amount of phrasing in this declaration—such as the pledge to use 'lawful means' to reverse the Supreme Court decision—can dim the hatred and open defiance of law and order poorly hidden within."

It was the season of presidential primary elections, and

neither President Eisenhower, who was preparing to run for a second term, nor any of the Republican members of Congress seemed eager to challenge the manifesto; they were silent at first, and then cautiously noncommittal. Of the seven Southern Republicans who then belonged to the House of Representatives, four signed the manifesto. (One of the four, Richard Poff of Virginia, was later nominated by President Nixon to fill the "Southern" seat on the Supreme Court.)

Among Southern Democrats, the pressure to sign and support the document was intense, and all but three senators and twenty-two representatives cooperated. In the House, seventeen of the twenty-one members from Texas (one of them a Republican) refused to sign, taking their cue from House majority leader Sam Rayburn. The only others who stood with them were four of Tennessee's eight representatives (two of them Republicans), three from North Carolina, and one from Florida. In the Senate, the only nonsigners were Albert Gore and Estes Kefauver of Tennessee (Kefauver, a candidate for President, said flatly, "I just don't agree with it"), and Lyndon Johnson of Texas.

Johnson, the Senate majority leader, had been suggested as a presidential candidate, and two of the principal figures in the drafting of the manifesto, Senators Richard Russell of Georgia and Strom Thurmond of South Carolina, had pledged him their support. But Johnson and Rayburn, with Kefauver and Gore and the others, stood their ground against the coercion of colleagues and constituents, and thus kept the South from presenting a united front against the authority of the Supreme Court. One among them was Representative Homer Thornberry of Texas, whom Johnson, when he was President, nominated to fill a vacancy on the Court.

Some of the South's liberals and moderates were unable to withstand the pressure on them. Among those who signed were Senators William Fulbright of Arkansas, Sam Ervin of North Carolina, and John Sparkman of Alabama, and Representatives Brooks Hays of Arkansas, Frank Smith of Mississippi, Ross Bass of Tennessee, and Hale Boggs of Louisiana.

Eight of the congressmen who did not sign the manifesto are still members of the House. Among the signers, eight senators and eighteen representatives are still in office. It has been a long time since any of them reminded their constituents of the part they played in one of the most serious threats to be raised against constitutional government in the United States since the Civil War. The failure of political leadership was a primary cause of the violence and destruction that scarred the mind and soul of the South in the ten years following the signing of the Southern Manifesto, and the men who put their names to that document share a heavy responsibility for the havoc. They set the example that Orval Faubus and George Wallace and Ross Barnett followed.

Some of the signers of the manifesto no doubt regret their involvement in that shameful episode. If their views have changed, so have those, apparently, of a prominent political figure who favored the Supreme Court decision and opposed the manifesto, and his actions then and now add a timely and telling footnote to the story.

A few days after the document was presented to Congress, a group of liberals launched a counterattack against it in the Senate. One of their leaders was Senator Herbert Lehman of New York, and after he had spoken, Senator Clifford Case, a New Jersey Republican, praised his remarks as "eloquent, deeply moving and sincere." But Case went on to chide Lehman for his charge that President Eisenhower hadn't offered adequate leadership in response to the manifesto, and he suggested that it would be better not to "bring politics" into the issue. Senator Richard Neuberger of Oregon, who stood with Lehman, was quick to respond.

"The man who put this matter into politics," Neuberger said, "is the Vice President of the United States, who referred to the Chief Justice of the United States [Earl Warren] as a Republican Chief Justice."

The Vice President was Richard M. Nixon. Eager to be retained for a second term as Eisenhower's running mate, he had sought to capitalize on a court decision he apparently perceived to be applicable only to a region where there were few Republican votes. He had praised the decision—and identified its author, Chief Justice Warren, as a member of his own political party.

And twelve years later, the same Richard Nixon was attacking the judicial record of the same Earl Warren, and making campaign promises to appoint justices to the Court whose decisions on race and crime and civil liberties would not be so "liberal."

He has tried his best to keep those promises. Louis M. Kohlmeier of the *Wall Street Journal*, writing in his book, *God Save This Honorable Court,* said "President Nixon's place in history is secure . . . [he has] politicized the Supreme Court more dramatically than any President in history." First with Clement Haynsworth and then with Harrold Carswell, he attempted to appoint Southern judges of mediocre caliber whose records gave cheer to segregationist whites in the South, and when the Senate rejected both of them, Nixon angrily and hypocritically accused the Senate of bias and discrimination against the South. He appointed Warren Burger as chief justice to replace Earl Warren, and when Burger authored a unanimous decision affirming the use of busing as a constitutionally permissible tool for achieving school desegregation, Nixon responded by stepping up his personal campaign against busing.

As he has politicized the court, so has he turned the issue of school desegregation and busing into a political football. When he claims that more school desegregation has taken place during his administration than in all the prior years back to 1954, he is taking credit for the results of court actions which he and his civil rights and justice department officials have made every effort to thwart. During his tenure, prosecution of school districts for noncompliance with the Civil Rights Act of

1964 has virtually ceased; federal funds to aid desegregating school districts have never materialized to the extent they were promised; funds for busing have been prohibited; and even the money he promised for compensatory education programs as an alternative to desegregation has not been forthcoming.

The Southern strategy of 1968, and its metamorphosis into the "new American majority" of 1972, incorporated the spirit, if not the letter, of the Southern Manifesto. Nixon has succeeded where Barry Goldwater failed, and he has stopped what Lyndon Johnson started. In order to capture the white South, he has promised it relief from the incursions of the black South, and he has extended that promise to the rest of white America: busing will not succeed; the suburbs will not be desegregated; loafers on the welfare rolls will be cut off; law and order will prevail; the Supreme Court will strengthen the peace forces against the crime forces.

It was enough to get him reelected by a landslide. And along the way, Nixon did not ignore the South; he simply courted it selectively. He rounded up enough black supporters to send a "Black Blitz" team through the region to campaign for him. Just before the election he declared a "National Country Music Week" for the benefit of the "silent majority," and later he invited country singer Merle Haggard to the White House to sing his "good ole boy" hit song "Okie from Muskogee." He spurned a Republican candidate for the Senate in Mississippi in order to support the reelection of supersegregationist James O. Eastland. He secured a multimillion-dollar federal loan for former civil rights activist Floyd McKissick, who is building a black "new town" in North Carolina. He let Sammy Davis, Jr., embrace him, John Connally endorse him, and Billy Graham bless him. And he completed his capture of the South by sending George Wallace's coded message out to the folks: When it comes to the crunch, it's gonna be *us* against *them*, and there's more of *us*, so vote for me and you won't have to worry.

Down on his ranch, LBJ viewed it all in silence. Whatever his assets and liabilities as President, Johnson was an activist on the domestic front, and his initiatives against poverty and racial discrimination were now the very programs Nixon seemed most eager to scuttle. In December 1972, a few weeks before he died, Johnson invited a group of civil rights leaders and officials of his administration to Austin for a symposium on the occasion of the opening of his civil rights papers to the public. It is an extensive and—by comparison, at least—an impressive record, containing about a million pages of legislation, correspondence, reports, and speeches. By contrast, the only speech Nixon made on race during his first term in office was a diatribe against busing. But Johnson didn't dwell on the contrast. He made a moving speech to his Texas guests about the unfinished business of assuring equal rights and justice for racial minorities, and he urged them to "get our folks to reasoning together" and take their case directly to Nixon. "The President wants to do what's right," he said. Most of his listeners seemed unconvinced.

When he was nearing the end of his administration and the Vietnam morass had all but consumed him, Johnson found to his frustration and dismay that his domestic policies were also being criticized. He was bitter about it, and his critics were equally embittered. But during those two days in Texas, most of that was forgiven and forgotten. Roy Innis, the black nationalist leader of CORE and a sometime trader in the Nixon camp, made an unscheduled speech that drew a charge of "black demagoguery" from one of his brothers, but Johnson played his Great Reconciler role to the end. And when it was over, Georgia state legislator and black activist Julian Bond offered a summary observation. Johnson, he said, "is a human-hearted man, and, oh, God, do I wish he was there [in the White House] now."

So must a good many other Americans, in and out of the South. In the wake of his reelection, Richard Nixon was able to savor for a few months the sweet taste of total victory, and in that short time he may have possessed more raw power than any President in American history. Had he known how short-lived it would be, he might have considered engineering a military coup to perpetuate his rule. But too late: the Watergate ruptured, and in the ensuing flood the President's ship of state ran aground. The revelations of Watergate and other related scandals are too recent to permit anything more than a preliminary body count, but it seems likely that Nixon's "new American majority" has died aborning, at least as far as his paternity is concerned. His personal credibility, which was never great even at the height of his power, is now all but irreparably destroyed. What effect the scandals will have on the American political system—and, incidentally, on such matters as race relations and the vaunted Southern strategy—must remain for others to assess after the flood.

The President may owe a large measure of his post-election catastrophe to his approach to politics as a high-stakes football game between the good guys and the bad guys. He attracted to his "team" the sort of politicians, businessmen, militarists, athletes, and religionists who prize victory above all else, and they responded to their "coach" with certitude and zeal and a devotion bordering on fanaticism. Winning has been the name of the President's game. Dedication and concentration and self-righteousness and piety and pitilessness have characterized his style. He has been vindictive in victory and defiant in defeat. But he has failed to learn a fundamental lesson from the world of sports: Sooner or later a team with all the advantages is going to get beat, even if it cheats.

While Johnson was in the White House, he was the South's prime export to the national political arena, and he left a sizable imprint. The next most influential Southerner on the national scene has been George Wallace, and but for the insanity of Arthur Bremer, he might still be within reach of the presidency. On election night in 1972, NBC's David Brinkley said Nixon had won an overwhelming victory because "he more accurately reflects the mood of the country, the mood best expressed by George Wallace."

It was not the race issue alone that catapulted Wallace to prominence, but there is no doubt that it has been his sword and his cymbal. Doomed to also-ran status on the American party ticket, he returned to the Democrats in 1972 and rode the school busing controversy to victory in half a dozen primaries, driving the other Democratic candidates up the wall in the process.

The Wallace phenomenon says a lot about the South and the nation. Until the campaign of 1968, Wallaceism was a relatively small movement of Southern whites and upcountry allies struggling to retain white supremacy. But the nation's growing alarm over racial issues that were no longer confined to the South, and Nixon's own reaction to those fears, gave Wallace an opportunity and an audience, and he made the most of them.

From his earliest involvement in politics to his emergence as a serious candidate for the presidency, Wallace made an early about-face—from racial moderation to white supremacy—and a succession of subsequent adjustments that had more to do with style than substance. He got more mileage out of the school desegregation issue than any other, and in that area he shifted with the tide of white sentiment—from ardent and unyielding segregation to "freedom of choice" to "neighborhood schools" and resistance to busing.

Still, it would be too simplistic to attribute all of Wallace's popularity to his busing stand, or even to his overall attitude on race. He is an intelligent man, a shrewd and agile politician, and he has enlarged his following by enlarging his list of grievances and by modifying his public positions on some racial issues. His following is still virtually all white, but that fact is downplayed. He has professed to speak for "the little man," "the average American," the working man–union member–farmer–merchant–cab driver. Many thousands of whites who are intimidated and victimized by bigness—big government, big business, big labor unions, big educational networks, big religious bodies, big cities—have responded to him because he has articulated so specifically their fears and their anger. With allowances for individual differences, the main body of his support has come from people who think of themselves as "conservative" and "old-fashioned." They are for patriotism, tough discipline, a strong military, hard work, prayer, religious piety, tax relief, neighborhood schools, capital punishment, male dominance, white dominance, middle-class dominance. They are against welfare, special privileges for the rich, gun control, permissiveness, amnesty, abortion, long hair, sexual freedom, marijuana, women's liberation, black power, government regulation, intellectuals, the arrogant rich. They are anticommunist, antisocialist, antifederalist, antiintegrationist. All the people who have affluence and influence, the people who control things from above the grime of daily battle, are common foes: bankers, industrialists, labor union czars, big politicians, civil rights leaders, university professors, foundation executives, people who dominate the media. The Wallaceites harbor a particular resentment against people who favor integration but send their kids to private schools, those who are opposed to war and yet condone a class-discriminatory military draft system, those who favor punishment for William Calley but acquittal for Muhammad Ali and amnesty for the young men who fled to Canada, those who are against capital punishment but for abortion, those who are for integrated housing while living in neighborhoods economically beyond the reach of most blacks and all poor people, those who worry about prison reform without ever having to worry about being sentenced to jail, and those who want to liberalize laws on drugs and abortion—if only to legitimize what they have long done discreetly and anonymously, safe from prosecution.

In this catalog of grievances there is some truth and logic, and also some contradiction and oversimplification. It is broad enough to encompass some of the philosophies of Nixon and Goldwater, some of the points that Robert Kennedy and George McGovern made in their campaigns, and even a few of the things Martin Luther King and Malcolm X used to talk about. But George Wallace does not fit comfortably in any of those camps. Nixon and Goldwater are too rich, too slick, too much a part of the industrial-political establishment; Kennedy and McGovern had too much support from liberals and radicals and intellectuals; King and Malcolm were too black. Wallace has pursued a different course; he has chosen selectively those things which most frighten and frustrate the masses of white Middle Americans, and he has hammered away at them incessantly. And the people who want women and blacks and young people back in their places, the nation back to its World War II supremacy, the corporate fat cat back in line, the corner grocery back on the corner, prices back to normal, and everybody back in church have cheered on the feisty little prize fighter from Alabama each time he has taken the fight to one of the foes. What he would do if he were President has mattered little; for most of his followers, it has been satisfying enough just to listen to him rail against the high and the mighty. George could promise them more discipline in the home and school, more punishment in the courts, more authority for the police, and more retaliation against sex, sin, smut, and subversion—and just the promise was enough. And finally, there was the message about blacks, the message Nixon appropriated from him; it was the basis for all else, the adhesive element in Wallace's appeal.

So he has become a fixture on the American political scene, and even in his wheelchair he cannot be counted out; Roosevelt rode one to the top, he reminds questioners. Unless he loses his power base in Alabama or is forced for physical reasons to retire from politics, he will continue to personify for millions of Americans a Southern reaction to the nation's malaise. And in the hope that he may get another chance, he has even hand-picked a few blacks to help him overcome his racist image. One of them is Norman E. Jones, a Floridian who wants to write a book called *Black Man for Wallace*. Jones was in the Florida delegation at the 1972 Democratic National Convention in Miami Beach, and he led four other black delegates to bolt from the McGovern camp and support Wallace. "I'm proud to be an Uncle Tom," Jones told a reporter. "An Uncle Tom is a shrewd and smooth diplomat. During slavery days, the Uncle Toms were the black servants who were smart enough to wheedle and charm their way into the white master's confidence. . . . Blacks have managed to survive in this nation all these years by being Uncle Toms." Later, to another writer, Jones indicated where he thought the current of American politics was going. "The trend is to the right," he said. "I saw that ten years ago. I want others to get in the boat now, or else there are going to be a lot of drowned niggers."

Jones is about as close to being a typical black Southerner as Wallace is to winning a brotherhood award from the NAACP. Increasing thousands of blacks in the region have become active in politics since the Voting Rights Act was passed in 1965, and they have had an impact on the two major parties, on third-party movements, and as independents, but the number who are supporters of Wallace could only be described as minuscule. The dramatic increase in registered black voters and in black elected officials throughout the South has caused white politicians—Wallace among them—to abandon openly racist appeals for votes, and with the passage of time, black political power in the region may influence the pace and direction of change more profoundly than Wallace could at the height of his power. If Wallace is a symbol to the nation of continuing white racism in the South, black political strength is a countersymbol of incipient racial equality.

In 1965, only seventy-two blacks held elective offices in the eleven Southern states; after the 1972 elections, the number had risen to 1,144. Included in the total are two members of Congress, six state senators, fifty-five state representatives, ninety county commissioners, thirty-eight mayors, 422 city councilmen, nine judges, ten sheriffs and marshals, and 259 school board members. The increase of 271 in 1972 alone was the largest in any single year since Reconstruction. Mississippi, which had no black elected officials in 1965, had 145 at the beginning of 1973—more than any other Southern state. Almost half of all the black elected officials in the nation are Southern officeholders.

When the Southern Regional Council in Atlanta set up the Voter Education Project (VEP) in 1961, only about one-fourth of the black voting age population was registered, but by 1973, about 60 percent of all eligible blacks were registered—in round figures, 3,750,000 people. In about one hundred Southern counties, the black voting age population is greater than the white, and in five of those counties, a majority of local government elected officials are black. Selma, Alabama, offers one especially illustrative example of the changing political picture. It was in Selma in 1965 that a wave of state and local police officials swept into a line of blacks marching to dramatize the denial of their right to vote. More than fifty people were seriously injured, and the brutality of that assault jolted Congress into quick passage of the Voting Rights Act. Less than 3 percent of the black voting age population in Selma and surrounding Dallas County was registered to vote at that time; in 1972, two-thirds of the age-eligible black population was registered, and five blacks were elected to the ten-seat city council. One of the black marchers who was seriously injured in that bloody event at Selma in 1965 was John Lewis, chairman of SNCC, the civil rights group. Lewis is now the executive director of the Voter Education Project.

More examples can be cited of the impact of blacks on Southern politics, and the consequent effect on whites. Half a dozen or more of the black mayors in the South preside over majority-white constituencies; Andrew Young's congressional district in Atlanta is 62 percent white; Barbara Jordan of Houston owes her congressional victory to a coalition of blacks, whites, and Chicanos; black delegates to the Democratic National Convention in 1972 numbered 450—15 percent of the total—and they made up almost twice that percentage in the delegations of the Southern states; blacks now hold sixteen legislative seats in Georgia, twenty-six county commissioner posts in Louisiana, sixty-four city governing board seats in North Carolina, fifty-five law enforcement positions in Alabama, and forty-nine school board seats in Arkansas.

"The rate of increase in the number of black elected officials in the South has been phenomenal," the president of VEP, Harry Huge, said when the agency released its tabulations in 1973. "It reflects the very basic fact that the momentum for change generated by the civil rights movement of the 1960s continues to shape the political, social, and economic climate of our region." And John Lewis added: "Such victories restore faith in the political process and keep alive our dreams for a positive transformation of the Southern region."

But Lewis acknowledges that the changes, however impressive, show only one side of the political coin; the other side is not so encouraging. There are more than 1,100 black officeholders in the South, but there are almost 80,000 elective offices, and the black share is thus less than 2 percent; almost 60 percent of the age-eligible black population in the region is registered—leaving 40 percent, or about 2.5 million people, unaffected by the changes; and in every Southern state but two, the percentage of age-eligible whites who are registered exceeds the black percentage.

Furthermore, the rate of increase in black voter registration has begun to fall as a result of a combination of factors, including laxness in federal enforcement of the Voting Rights Act, continued intimidation of black voters and would-be voters in many areas of the rural South, the cumbersome and complex makeup of most voter registration systems, and the numbing effect of a century of exclusion on hundreds of thousands of potential black voters.

One further disquieting note should be mentioned. In the decade of Reconstruction following the Civil War, more than a million blacks registered to vote, and they elected twenty representatives and two senators to Congress and a multitude of officials to state offices. When federal troops were withdrawn from the South in 1877 by President Rutherford B. Hayes, black political rights were wiped out; by 1902, no blacks were left in Congress, not a single state legislature in the nation had even one black member, and black voter registration in the South fell almost to rock bottom. Legal and extralegal manipulation, intimidation, and fraud stripped Southern blacks of all but the barest pretense of their political rights, and in the North, less blatant behavior on the part of whites produced a similar result.

The specter of a return to segregation and disfranchisement and other injustices characteristic of the post-Reconstruction period may be overdrawn, but it has been raised time and time again since President Nixon took office.

When he arrived in Congress to begin his first term in January 1973, Andrew Young told a reporter for the *Christian Science Monitor* that the black politician is replacing the civil rights leader as the spearpoint of black progress. He said the increasing involvement of blacks in the political process is fostering a reassessment of attitudes on the part of Southern whites, and it is also indicative "that blacks generally have decided that their lot is cast with America."

The effect of black political power on white attitudes can be measured to some extent at the ballot box, and Young's own case offers a good illustration. It can also be measured in the words and actions of Southern white politicians. Every Southern governor, even Wallace, now treads more gingerly than in the past when dealing with racial issues. A few of them have spoken candidly about the need for affirmative action to eliminate segregation and the lingering vestiges of white supremacy, and at least a couple—Reubin Askew of Florida and Linwood Holton of Virginia—have done more than talk. And the black voters, in responding to these signs of change, have shown considerable political sophistication: they have followed the man rather than the party, giving Republicans Holton and, earlier, Winthrop Rockefeller of Arkansas as much allegiance as they gave Askew and others on the Democratic side. In Alabama, where neither party has shown much interest in reaching equitable accommodations with black voters, the National Democratic party of Alabama, an independent, biracial third party (more accurately, a fourth party, until Wallace returned to the Democratic fold), has been responsible for much of the success blacks have had in getting elected to local offices. The best example of that is in Greene County, where a black population approaching 80 percent elected black candidates to most of the county's offices in 1969 and 1970, and did it with the help of the NDPA. Blacks now occupy the sheriff's office, the county judge's office, and most of the seats on the school board and the county commission. A few whites have remained in office. When he was sworn in in January 1971, Sheriff Thomas Earl Gilmore stood beside his deputies—two blacks, one white—and said Greene County "is the beginning of a new hope for America."

Greene County has not been transformed into a model of racial amity and economic prosperity since that passing of the torch. It is one of the South's poorest rural counties. Some whites have left, and others have divorced themselves from any involvement in politics—and whites still control most of what little economic power there is. But the black elected officials have shown themselves to be at least as capable of running the government as their white predecessors were. As they gain more experience, and as the whites who remain recover from the trauma of losing their political grip, Greene County has a good chance to become a responsive and effective governmental unit—and for most of its citizens, it has never been that.

So the cross-fertilization of political life continues between the South and the nation, and between the blacks and whites of the South. And in the Southwest, Chicano political power adds still another dimension: in Texas in 1972, party regulars were jarred from their siesta by the sound of voters marching to the beat of La Raza Unida, a Chicano third-party movement.

The influences taken North by Southerners—Lyndon Johnson, George Wallace, Andrew Young, Barbara Jordan, scores of state and local black and Chicano elected officials, the women's movement—mix and mingle and clash with one another and with the influences being shipped to the South by Northerners—Richard Nixon, the Republican party, the Democratic party, more waves of politically awakened women. Populism, a political movement with a Jekyll-Hyde image a century old, came out of hibernation in the 1972 campaign, and its principal advocate was Senator Fred Harris of Oklahoma, son of a Mississippi-born sharecropper. Analyses of the voting records of Southerners in Congress show that as the South urbanizes, its political representatives become more urban than Southern. They no longer present a solid and monolithic front as they did in the days of the Southern Manifesto, not even on racial issues.

To all of this has now been added the Watergate scandal. The Southern strategy that brought President Nixon to the pinnacle of a new Solid South in 1972 has been overshadowed by the spectacle of a massive breakdown of law and order in the White House itself. (Ironically, the two most prominent figures in the Senate investigation of Watergate are Southerners—Sam Ervin, a North Carolina Democrat, and Howard Baker, a Tennessee Republican—and two other members of the seven-man investigating committee are also Southerners.)

There is turbulence and instability and uncertainty in American political life now, and the South is very much a part of it. In all of the new alliances and coalitions and splinterings, in the revelations of high-level corruption and the crisis of confidence, all bets are off: In the summer of 1973, nothing was certain—not the Southern strategy, not even four more years of Nixon. Nobody has a handle on "the American Majority."

Cities: Recreating the Monster Metropolis

One of the most publicized and most promising developments in American urbanization in recent years has been the rise of new towns—planned communities in which creative and unconventional approaches to urban living are encouraged and enhanced by the opportunity to start afresh in a setting unmarred by past failures. Perhaps the best-known such community is Columbia, Maryland, in the fast-developing corridor between Baltimore and Washington.

It is one of those interesting little coincidences of history that 180 years before the beginning of Columbia, Maryland, the legislature of South Carolina voted to move that state's capitol from Charleston to one of the first planned communities in the nation's history—and it named that new town Columbia. Four square miles of plantation land were laid out in city blocks divided by broad avenues 100 to 150 feet wide, and a

151

spacious site near the center was set aside for the construction of the capitol building. And from that beginning in 1785, Columbia, South Carolina, has developed into one of the 100 largest metropolitan centers in the United States: In 1970, there were 323,000 people living in what the Census Bureau calls the "standard metropolitan statistical area" of the city, ranking it ninety-first in size among the nation's SMSAs.

The state capitol and those wide boulevards surrounding it form an impressive centerpiece for downtown Columbia today. The State House, as the capitol is called, is an imposing domed structure, a massive granite edifice that rises above the towering live oaks around it like some ancient Roman hall of honor. Two blocks up Sumter Street is the University of South Carolina, almost as old as the city itself. Buildings of the state government and the university, churches, ancient homes, and other historic structures—and a venerable cemetery just across the avenue from the State House—dominate "old Columbia," the original "new town," and the charm of it is enhanced by the shady live oaks and the prodigious banks of azaleas that bloom in such profusion every spring. Far from being beyond restoration, as so many core cities are, downtown Columbia is an attractive and inviting place, convenient and accessible, and it is easy to imagine working and living there comfortably.

Beyond the four square miles of symmetrical city blocks and straight avenues, the urban community sprawls over 200 square miles of the South Carolina Midlands, laced with highways and railroads, sprinkled with subdivisions and shopping centers and industrial complexes. It is a thriving, hustling, promising city, with assets sufficient to encourage complacency. And it is also a troubled city, faced with problems it may lack the skill—and the will—to resolve. The promise predominates now; Columbia is not a city racked with crisis, and the prevailing mood there is optimistic. But its problems are the familiar ones that plague cities all over America, and though there are Columbians who feel a sense of urgency about facing them while they are still manageable, most people do not seem to share that view.

By almost every economic and statistical index, metropolitan Columbia measures healthy. Population, personal income, industrial payrolls, retail sales, and new construction all registered big gains in the 1960s, and the national recession hardly slowed the pace at all: growth has continued almost undeterred in the 1970s. The city has a diversified economy that includes large industrial and manufacturing firms and a U.S. Army base (Fort Jackson) as well as its governmental and higher educational enterprises. It is the leading wholesale and retail commercial center of the state. It has a moderate climate, a relatively low crime rate, tolerable traffic conditions, an unemployment rate below the national average, below-average taxes and living costs, adequate cultural and recreational facilities, passably decent health service, a good water supply, enough churches and synagogues to meet the demand, a lot of friendly and hospitable people, and telephones that work. The Greater Columbia Chamber of Commerce, in a "facts and figures" booklet that sometimes slips into subjective hyperbole, calls Columbia "One of the Greatest Cities of America's Future." The booklet identifies "Our citizens' motto" as "An honest day's work for an honest day's pay," and it boasts three times in its twenty pages that only 4 percent of the labor force in the metropolitan area is unionized. That dubious distinction aside, the surface impression a visitor is apt to get is that Columbia is a nice place to live and work, a "good city" as cities go.

And then there is the other side—the problems and troubles and deficiencies that chamber of commerce brochures never mention. In 1970, the Central Midlands Regional Planning Council published an analysis of the social, economic, and physical environment of the Columbia urban area. Dividing the community into 122 neighborhoods, the council measured each one against a set of "blight indices"—family income, welfare cases, arrests, tuberculosis cases, venereal disease cases, substandard or dilapidated or deteriorating housing, incompatible mixtures of land use, fire halls, water and sewer systems, and unpaved streets. Thirty-two of the neighborhoods are predominantly industrial or institutional or commercial, and have few residents; of the ninety others, twenty-three showed a serious degree of blight in six or more of the twelve indices—and in all but two of these seriously blighted neighborhoods, blacks made up at least two-thirds of the population. Only four of the twenty-five neighborhoods having a majority-black population showed a relatively low degree of blight.

The planning council noted in its study that family income is the most direct index of the overall quality of a neighborhood's environment, since all of the other blight factors are related to it. In none of the majority-black areas did most of the families earn more than $8,500 a year, and in thirteen of the twenty-five black neighborhoods, most of the families were shown to earn less than $3,600 a year.

Poverty and discrimination—and all of their attendant social and environmental problems—are brought into sharp focus by the planning council study. Columbia does not project an image of blatant white supremacy the way it once did, but it still lives with the consequences of that ideology, and it has made few significant strides toward the eradication of those consequences: Most of its poor are black, most of its housing is segregated—and most of its unpaved streets, its substandard housing, its health problems, its arrests, and its welfare cases are in the segregated areas where blacks live. In the city's public schools, the circumstances are different, but the lingering consequences of discrimination are still apparent: In 1968, before the schools were desegregated, their enrollment was about 45 percent black; by the fall of 1972, they were 56 percent black, and the familiar process of resegregation could be measured in the white flight to private schools and suburban school districts. The city's official population figures disguise the extent of white flight. Columbia's city proper showed an increase of 16,000 people—from 97,000 to 113,000 —between 1960 and 1970, but annexation more than accounted for the growth. In the geographical area on which the 1960 census was based, the population by 1970 had actually declined by more than 12,000.

However much racial issues predominate in metropolitan Columbia's preoccupation with contemporary problems, they are by no means the only serious concern. Zoning, taxation, public transportation, streets and highways, parking, pollution, drainage and sewers, police protection, and employment opportunities are also issues that beg for attention, and while measurable improvement has been made in most of those areas, the pace of change is exceeded by the demand for it. And as in most cities, programs of freeway construction, urban renewal, and public housing in Columbia have often been a mixed blessing at best, and a disruptive and divisive influence at worst.

Almost all of these problems, including the racial ones, have been exacerbated by one overriding difficulty: the fragmentary, duplicative, and confusing pattern of local government organization. There is, to begin with, the city of Columbia, which has a mayor, a manager, and a council. Then there is the Richland County Council—Richland County being the political jurisdiction in which the city of Columbia is located. Also in Richland County are the incorporated municipalities of Forest Acres and Arcadia Lakes—the latter covering one square mile of land—and the Fort Jackson military base. Just across the Congaree River, which flows barely half a mile west of the State House, is Lexington County—very much a part of the Columbia urban area—and in Lexington County are the incorporated towns of West Columbia, Cayce, and Springdale. And in addition to all this, there are four public school districts in the urban area—two in each county—and there is a confusing and seemingly endless overlap of public services: fire departments, police departments, water systems, drainage districts, road departments, taxing and zoning authorities, garbage collection departments, licensing authorities. To confuse matters further, much power over local government is exercised by state legislators representing the two counties: Richland County's fourteen-member legislative delegation and Lexington County's smaller contingent not only are central to the local lawmaking and administrative processes; they are also the de facto chiefs of the political machinery.

There is nothing unique about the hodgepodge of legislative and administrative jurisdictions in metropolitan Columbia— cities everywhere, large and small, have similar patterns—and there is no mystery about how and why they came to be. Since Columbia was a new town, it has grown and spread, and its growth has been random and unplanned and uncoordinated. The resulting duplication and conflict are not unlike what happened in St. Louis and Baltimore and Philadelphia decades ago—or what is happening in Birmingham and Atlanta now.

In the 1972 elections, Richland County voters overwhelmingly defeated a proposal calling for limited consolidation of governmental functions in the city and county. A special study commission in Columbia had spent months looking into the legal ramifications of such a merger, but its recommendations were rejected, even though the commission did not even consider the issue of school district consolidation, and it did not get into the question of merger between Richland and Lexington counties. Comprehensive urban consolidation, then, was not even at issue—and the margin of defeat for the modest proposal on the ballot suggests that it will not be for a long time to come. In short, urban consolidation is not in the cards in Columbia now—and that means it may never be, because the complexities of such a merger will multiply as the city grows.

On some issues, intergovernment cooperation has been successful. There is a modern airport facility in Lexington County serving the entire metropolitan area, and a comprehensive plan for the location of interstate highways and urban freeways has moved into the development stage. But those are the exceptions. The controversial issues—public housing, schools, zoning, police protection—show little promise of comprehensive resolution. Natural competitiveness and a reluctance to change familiar patterns are a partial explanation, but the most serious obstacles have to do with race and class, and in its handling of those issues Columbia is moving in the same direction its Northern sister cities moved long ago.

Richland School District One is now majority-black; District Two, in the suburbs, is about 85 percent white. Yet the population of the city of Columbia is only one-third black, and the rest of Richland County is also one-third black. (Lexington County's black population is only 13 percent, and its school districts are close to 90 percent white.) And if the disparities in these percentages reflect a widening racial gap between the city of Columbia and its suburbs in Richland County, there is another more subtle gap separating Richland and Lexington counties. White leaders on the Richland side of the river manifest a tendency to view Lexington as "the other side of the tracks"—less progressive, less enlightened, albeit predominantly white. This attitudinal division is resented in Lexington County, but the resentment does not lessen the feeling of superiority many Columbians apparently harbor. "The big money is over here," a Columbia political leader observed, "and money is power."

So metropolitan Columbia is split not only by the river and the county line and the myriad of municipalities; it is even more divided by race and class and economics and attitudes. The divisions are not as clear-cut as they were in the days of legalized segregation, but they are, if anything, far more complicated. There is movement and change where there was not much before, but the relative positions and conditions of blacks in particular and low-income people in general have not improved very much. The District One school system, struggling to adjust to desegregation and white flight and a growing black majority, offers a good illustration of Columbia's resemblance to the cities of the North.

Hayes Mizell is a white man in his middle thirties who serves on the District One school board. A native Southerner, he has been the director since 1966 of the South Carolina Community Relations Program of the American Friends Service Committee, and in his job as well as in his school board role, he is a plain-spoken advocate of complete racial integration. He came to Columbia the same year the civil rights movement lost the spotlight and the South lost the stage—the year Black Power and the Northern cities seized America's attention —and he has been, in a curious way, an anomalous figure, almost an anachronism, since the day he arrived.

Not many people, white or black, spend all their time working for racial integration and human equality in the South anymore—or, for that matter, outside the South either. There is the Urban League, of course, and the NAACP, and there is the remnant of the Southern Christian Leadership Conference, but the nature and extent of their involvements have changed. The Legal Defense Fund and the American Friends Service Committee are two biracial national organizations still playing an activist role in the pursuit of justice for minorities at the grass-roots level in the South. The Southern Regional Council and the Voter Education Project—the latter a spinoff from the former—are the best-known and most active indigenous organizations engaged in what are essentially integrationist activities. But the legions of marchers and supporters are gone, and the ones who remain, the whites and blacks who keep plugging away at the inequities in "the System," are a special breed. In a nation and a region long since weary of civil rights and integration, in a time of separatism and nationalism and ersatz equality, they are still pursuing the genuine article: a society which no longer gives special advantages to its white and wealthy citizens, at the expense of all others.

Mizell is one of those pluggers, one of the professional integrationists. When he was elected to the school board in 1970,
Columbia's morning newspaper, *The State*, sounded the editorial alarm that "a double-dipped integrationist long active in
civil rights causes" had just unseated the long-time chairman
of the school board. Since then, hardly a week has passed
without some mention in the press of Mizell and his manifold
school integration activities. He has been assailed in speeches,
resolutions, and letters to the editor, accused of being a white
extremist, a leftist agitator, a wrecker of South Carolina. Two
governors, a couple of congressmen, several state legislators,
and an assortment of local officials have aimed accusatory
barbs at him, and he has returned their fire with unblinking
truculence.

Columbia is a city which has long nourished a self-image of
moderate reasonableness. Even in its segregationist days it was
big on paternalism and gentility, and it considered deviations
from what it perceived to be the middle of the road as simply a
display of bad manners. Mizell, in that atmosphere, has been a
notorious and controversial character. Yet it is a measure of
his effectiveness that he kindles the rage and commands the
respect of segregationists and separatists alike, that he has a
high degree of credibility among blacks, and that his influence
exceeds his power by a considerable degree.

Mrs. Modjeska Simkins, a black woman long active in
Columbia civil rights battles, ran for the school board with
Mizell in 1968, and both of them lost. Since his subsequent
election, she has been one of his strongest supporters. "I have
a very high regard for him," she says. "He's taken a lot of
licks, but he has stood up to the reactionaries in education. I
call him every now and then to see if he's still in one piece.
Black people who know him have faith in him and admire him.
He's never taken an apologetic stand. There's nothing I can
say against him. He's all wool and a yard wide."

Lincoln Jenkins, an attorney and the only black on the

school board before elections for five of the seven school board seats were held in 1972, said of his colleague that some blacks and many whites were suspicious of him "because it is difficult to accept the fact that here is a white man dedicated to protecting the rights of black people." Mizell, he added, "is interested in the rights of men, black or white."

The ability to convey that interest consistently and sincerely is probably the basic reason for Mizell's survival as an integration advocate in the "post-integration" era. He has concentrated on the single issue of school integration and kept himself well informed on the subject; he has avoided ideological culs-de-sac; he has spoken his mind freely and bluntly; and in the best Quaker tradition of the American Friends Service Committee, he has been stubborn and tenacious and persistent. For all the people who resist integration, whatever their reasons, Mizell has been too formidable an opponent to be ignored.

The public reaction to Mizell during his tenure as a school board member provides a crude barometer for measuring the shifts and subtleties of the school desegregation issue in Columbia. At the time he went on the board, many white Columbians were still hoping to be rescued from any further desegregation by President Nixon, who was by then speaking out regularly in favor of neighborhood schools and against busing. Since then—thanks in part to Mizell—the school board has desegregated almost all its schools, and what used to be undisguised resistance to desegregation has taken new forms. Hardly anyone openly advocates segregation anymore; indeed, the opposition is not even to desegregation, but to "massive busing," and "the decline of quality," and "the breakdown of discipline," and "the loss of public confidence in the schools."

To label all of Mizell's white opponents as racists and segregationists would be to oversimplify the picture. The issue is no longer segregation versus desegregation. The concerns and preoccupations now are *re*segregation, white flight, white fright, the clash of cultures, the consequences of isolation, the conflict between classes, the inexperience and incompetence of teachers and administrators, the effects of unconscious racism, the use and misuse of standardized tests, the pros and cons of ability grouping, the impetuous hostility of children under pressure.

Something is happening in Columbia—something not unlike what is happening in cities all over the nation—that confuses and frustrates and discourages people, segregationists and integrationists and separatists alike. There are so many manifestations of the malaise that it is almost impossible to describe it, but what is happening is something like this: desegregation has arrived, but inequality persists, and so do friction and hostility and discord. Neither those who sought the demise of segregation nor those who resisted it are pleased with what is now taking place. The worth of public schools— their effectiveness, their quality, their very purpose—is being questioned and criticized by blacks and whites, the poor and the middle class and the well-to-do. Desegregation of the schools has not ushered in an era of equality and good feeling, far from it; on the contrary, it has exposed dimensions of inequality in the larger society that segregation kept insulated from public consciousness. In Columbia, as in other American communities North and South, large and small, it is white people with money who have most of the privileges and advantages, and they are fighting to defend that status against incursions from blacks, other minorities, and the poor in general. The racism in that struggle is subtle, latent. What most whites seem to want is a sort of cease-fire in place, a truce that ends the old style of discrimination but makes no allowances for the cumulative effects of that discrimination. So they oppose busing, and insist on neighborhood schools, and when those efforts fail they flee to private schools. And the black response becomes one of disillusionment with integration on white terms, and a deepening hostility toward whites.

Still, it is more complex than all that. There are whites who think desegregation is important and necessary, yet who feel what is happening to their children in school now is harming them, harming their chances to get a good education and go to a good college. There are former white segregationists whose children now get along well with black children in the schools. There are blacks who oppose busing, and send *their* children to private schools. There are, in short, almost as many moods and attitudes as there are people, and if they come close to agreeing on any one thing, it is that the schools are somehow not doing what they should do, not being what they should be. They should be teaching values—or they shouldn't. They should be preparing children for college, or for work, or for a full, well-rounded life. They should take sex education out, or put Bible reading and prayers back in, or administer more discipline, or less. They should make children cut their hair, or let them wear it long. They should tell them what to wear, or let them dress however they please. They should be offering Chinese and Russian and Latin and Swahili, or they should drop foreign languages. They should have special programs in black studies, or incorporate the black experience into existing courses, or ignore it altogether. There is no agreement on what is wrong with schools, on what they should be or do—but there is something approaching a consensus that they are unsatisfactory as they are.

When he was outside the structure of the schools, criticizing their segregation and their overall ineffectiveness, Hayes Mizell did not have as much visibility as he has now. Now he is, for better or worse, a part of the system, and what he says and does gets more exposure than it used to. He is no less a critic than he used to be, but he is more aware now that, in his words, "citing a problem and having an answer for it are two different things."

In the 1972 elections, five Republicans ran as a team for the available school board seats, and though Mizell was not up for reelection, he was the principal issue of the campaign. The Republicans had a single objective: "To save our public schools from a complete Mizell takeover." They won lopsided victories over three incumbents—including Lincoln Jenkins— and two other Democrats, and they promised to restore discipline and order and work for a return to neighborhood schools, the implication being that Mizell was primarily responsible for having kept these things from happening.

"I was a true believer too, before I went on the board," Mizell said before the election. "If those guys get elected, what they're gonna be impressed with are the limitations of power."

Soon after they took office, the new Republican majority tabled a proposed study of resegregation in the system by an out-of-town firm—a study for which Mizell had secured private funds. Early in 1973, Dr. Claud Kitchens, the beleaguered superintendent of schools, announced his resignation. The Columbia schools were firmly in the hands of a new team. Mizell, with two years remaining in his term of office, was philosophical about his role and his effectiveness, before and after the Republicans took over. "I think I recognize the limitations of who I am and where I'm coming from and what it is I can do," he said. "I have a better understanding of the sham of the system and people's bitterness toward it than I had before I was elected, but I guess I'm rooted in the middle-class belief that the American system has some peculiar ability to survive and to change."

Survival and change are the bedrock issues facing public education in Columbia now—not just in Richland District One but in the entire metropolitan area. The question is not whether Mizell or Kitchens or the school board's new majority or the black majority of school patrons or the white majority of taxpayers knows best how to run them, to make them work; the question is whether *anybody* can put together a school system that equitably and effectively serves all the people of Columbia. It is the same question Boston faces, and Atlanta, and St.

Louis, and scores of other cities. The continuing erosion of the public schools through discrimination, white flight, resegregation, internal strife and fiscal neglect suggests that the ultimate answer to the big question may be no more salutary for Columbia than for the other cities.

The Republican sweep of the school board in 1972 was also felt in some local government and legislative offices, and the Democratic party, which once had a well-entrenched machine and offered blacks some access to political power, found itself facing the perils of two-party politics for the first time. South Carolina also handed overwhelming reelection victories to President Nixon and Senator Strom Thurmond.

Neither Columbia's religious institutions nor its academic institutions have earned reputations as catalysts for racial and social and economic change in the city—they are not singled out for praise by liberals or for criticism by conservatives. The University of South Carolina has expanded its campus in recent years through urban renewal and the exercise of eminent domain, wiping out some rundown housing in the process, but if the university's expertise has been marshaled against the city's most pressing social problems, the evidence is not clearly visible. Two black institutions, Allen University and Benedict College, have been a source of pride to some blacks and a source of employment for others, but as agents of social change they have been hardly more engaged than the University of South Carolina. As for the churches and synagogues, they are present in large numbers but seldom mentioned as influential institutions in the realm of social issues.

In an indirect way, a religious institution has been instrumental in one particularly interesting local development, however. The United Presbyterian Church's South Carolina–Georgia Synod and its Board of National Missions have turned over 1,000 acres of church-owned land northwest of Columbia to a nonprofit development corporation for the construction of a new town. The town, to be called Harbison, will be a comprehensive community after the fashion of Columbia, Maryland. It is intended to provide housing, employment, and all the necessary supportive services for 21,000 people, and it will eventually cover more than 1,700 acres and involve a total investment of about $200 million in private and federal funds.

Harbison is being planned as a racially and economically integrated development. It has received strong support from some public and private agencies locally, as well as from the United Presbyterians and the U.S. Department of Housing and Urban Development. The project is in the charge of an interracial staff headed by two black men—a mortgage banker from Atlanta and an attorney from Washington. Inevitably, there are white realtors in Columbia who want to impose an image of low-income black suburbia on Harbison, but it should be regarded as a sign of community health that such an ambitious project could take root in Columbia, and some people are optimistic that it will succeed as an interracial development and influence broader changes in housing patterns elsewhere in the city.

The Greater Columbia Chamber of Commerce, which has been more active in efforts to end discrimination than chambers customarily are, announced a voluntary equal employment plan for the city in 1972, soon after a black organization threatened a boycott of downtown businesses to protest discrimination in hiring. The chamber plan is being directed by one of its affiliate divisions, the biracial Community Relations Council. Its goal is to raise the percentage of blacks in all types and levels of employment from about 15 percent overall in 1972 to about 35 percent by 1975. The plan also pledges to open up business opportunities for black entrepreneurs in shopping centers and in the downtown area, and provides for management training and job-placement services and a twice-a-year monitoring of progress. Local government bodies, the NAACP, the Urban League, and the Downtown Businessmen's

Association endorsed the plan. (In a progress report on the plan a year after its initiation, officials of the Community Relations Council said, "The plan as it stands now is inadequately financed to achieve its goals and business involvement also appears to be deficient.")

The chamber also initiated the development of a master plan for the long-range revitalization of Columbia's downtown district. Two Columbia-based planning agencies with involvements nationwide—Wilbur Smith and Associates and Lyles, Bissett, Carlisle & Wolff—joined with an international firm, Doxiadis Associates, to produce the master plan. Their final report, now called the Doxiadis Study, is a comprehensive blueprint for a thirty-year reconstruction of approximately the same area that made up the original town in the eighteenth century. Building on the existing base of governmental, commercial, educational, and historic structures, the plan blends restoration with new construction and includes such features as housing along the riverfront, a multilevel mall on Main Street, a transportation center, hotel and office expansion, civic and cultural buildings, parks, and light industry. (Excluded from the restoration plan was the Central Correctional Institution, South Carolina's maximum security prison. A Bastille-like structure more than a hundred years old, it sits behind granite walls on the banks of the Congaree River in downtown Columbia, and it has about 1,700 inmates in facilities built for 1,100. Like inmates everywhere, they complain of slave labor conditions, racism among officials, lack of adequate medical care, harsh discipline, and uncontrolled drug traffic.)

Like the Harbison project, the Doxiadis Study is not without its critics. As the suburban areas flourish, adding new subdivisions and shopping centers, and as commercial development increases in Lexington County across the river, downtown Columbia's commercial position weakens. Some influential businessmen are opposed to energizing the downtown area, preferring instead to wheel and deal on the suburban frontier.

And again, race and class enter the picture: Blacks and the poor of both races are a part of what downtown is, and they will be a part of what it becomes, and there are still many whites who cling to the hope that the suburbs will offer a permanent escape from that reality.

So Columbia moves, by fits and starts, into the complex world of urban problems and opportunities. The opportunities are measured in terms of time—time to save the urban core, to reverse the trend of racial division, to consolidate government services and strengthen the schools and raise economic levels. New initiatives such as Harbison and the Doxiadis Study and the equal employment plan are hopeful signs that Columbia could be wise enough to make what time it has count.

But the impediments to such a course are formidable. Residential and industrial growth in the outlying areas exacerbates the problems of transportation, pollution, and race-class division. Competition and duplication among political and governmental jurisdictions promises to become extravagant and unmanageable. The issues of race, class, finance, organization, and overall quality constitute a multiple crisis for the public schools, and there is practically nothing to encourage hope that the crisis can be averted.

"Columbia has not yet come to an either-or situation," one of the city's political leaders observed. "It's headed toward the same mistakes the big cities have made, but it hasn't arrived there yet, and it still has time. But there's no sense of urgency. We do a little and then feel proud, put out a fire and then relax. The style is low-key, casual, deliberate, subtle, polite, courteous, and passive. The aristocracy, the ruling class, says, 'Look how far we've come,' but not many people say, 'Look what we're doing to ourselves.' There are too many vested interests to control where we're headed, so nobody pushes, and the long-range problems and needs don't get serious attention until they become clear and present dangers, and then it's too late. This could be a great city—I hope someday it is—but it's

not now, and in many ways it's not even headed in that direction."

These glimpses of urban life in Columbia could just as
easily have come from more than a score of cities across the
South. The 1970 census showed 153 American cities with
100,000 or more inhabitants, and forty-six of them are in the
eleven Southern states—including ten in Texas and seven each
in Florida and Virginia. Thirteen of the fifty largest cities and
eleven of the fifty biggest standard metropolitan statistical
areas are in the South. Houston, Dallas, Atlanta, and Miami—
the region's four largest metropolitan centers—are among the
nation's twenty-five largest urban metropolises, and each of
them has more than 1,250,000 people.

In the fifty years between 1920 and 1970, the population of
the South doubled—from 25 million to 50 million. Urbanization during that period was even more rapid than overall
growth: only 25 percent of all Southerners lived in urban areas
in 1920; by 1970, almost 65 percent did. In Florida and
Texas, 80 percent of the people live in cities, and only in North
Carolina, South Carolina, and Mississippi do more people live
outside urban areas than in them.

In the biggest Southern cities, runaway growth has already
propelled them to the point where they resemble the giant
American metropolis in almost every particular. Houston and
Dallas and Atlanta sweep and sprawl in every direction, consuming countryside like a prairie fire; only the sea around
them keeps Miami and New Orleans from doing the same. Any
of these cities offers more to compare with New York or
Chicago or Los Angeles than Columbia does. Nevertheless,
Columbia is big enough to make the point: in America, where
the motto might well be "Grow or Die," urbanization is
unavoidable, irresistible, unstoppable, inevitable. It may also
be uncontrollable.

Joel Fleishman of Duke University, in a chapter on Southern cities published by the L. Q. C. Lamar Society in its 1972

book *You Can't Eat Magnolias,* asserts that the South still has time "to take hold of the energy of urbanization and shape it into more graceful, more humane, and more livable cities than those in other regions." He cites several ways in which South-ern cities are favorably different from their counterparts else-where: the region as a whole is still less metropolitan than other sections, its cities are comparatively smaller, they have less heavy industry, they are less decayed and deserted at the core, they have a thinner bureaucratic overlay, they are less densely populated, they are on the whole younger. These advantages are being eroded, says Fleishman, by two powerful national trends: the suburbanization of people (mostly whites) and jobs, and the ghettoization of racial minorities and the poor in the central cities. These trends are as pronounced in the South as they are elsewhere, but Fleishman sees some advantage remaining—if only, he says, "because we started later, and because we were poorer."

The South still has a little time, he says, and it still has an element of choice. How much time? "Time, for the South, is reduced to *now,*" he asserts. "We have about one generation. Twenty years." And what can be done? He lists four major things: control and order growth, finance education equally throughout each state, foster economic development in the black community, and desegregate. "Finally, and most urgently of all," he says, "we have got to attend directly to the matter at the heart of all our socioeconomic problems: racism."

Late in 1970, the deputy police superintendent of New Orleans, Louis J. Sirgo, made these remarks in a speech before a national honor society:

We have allowed our central city areas to deteriorate into slum housing for members of our national community who are at the bottom of our socioeconomic totem pole. . . . Do something for yourself this afternoon on your way home. Look closely at the area you are leaving for the police to handle, and think. . . . No, we can no longer hide our problems in prison cages, or federally subsidized low-rent housing developments, or in ghetto housing. I suggest that we begin to think about doing something about the responsibilities of the office which we hold, and if we don't, then the problem, like a contagious malady, will destroy us. . . . We must face up to our responsibility, and in facing up to this responsibility, we must also be prepared to deal with the greatest sin of American society, and that is the status of the American Negro. . . .

Two years later, in January 1973, a sniper barricaded in a high-rise motel in downtown New Orleans shot twenty-three people, killing six of them, before he was stopped. One of the people he killed was Louis Sirgo.

The mass killer in New Orleans was a black man, and his insane rampage was immediately labeled a "nationwide conspiracy," the opening blast of a black insurrection. That reaction prompted columnist Carl T. Rowan to write: "Few Americans seem to understand that the white majority in this country will never see itself in the wanton killings of Richard Speck, Charles Whitman or Charles Manson; to do so would be self-condemnation. But the tendency is always there for whites to see the entire black race in the criminal behavior of someone like that New Orleans sniper." The heart of all our problems, said Joel Fleishman, is racism.

"We have all heard it said that the South will solve its racial and urban problems before the North," Fleishman wrote. "I have said so myself, very smugly, especially to Northerners, but now I . . . must confess that while we have the margin required to solve our problems more easily, more quickly, and with less cost than the North, there is absolutely no evidence that we have been or are now using that margin constructively. What data we have suggest that we are blindly following the North down the path which has led it to its present disaster."

The mind turns back to Columbia. The University of South Carolina's Bureau of Urban and Regional Affairs conducted a citizen survey in 1971 on the qualities of urban life in Columbia, and found that blacks rated seven qualities significantly lower than whites: social problems and racial attitudes, job opportunities, the friendliness of people, shopping convenience, housing, access to outdoor recreation facilities, and churches. Whites and blacks rated the quality of the schools precisely the same: barely satisfactory. Pollster Louis Harris, in a 1972 survey in South Carolina, found that 65 percent of the people considered attracting new industry more important than preserving the environment. About seven of every ten blacks he questioned said there is racial discrimination in employment in the state; about six of every ten whites said there isn't. Governor John West said in 1973 that he is proud of South Carolina's "unique race relations, which are second to none in the nation," and he added, "We can guarantee prospective industrialists that we have no racial problems in South Carolina."

Columbia: the 188-year-old planned community. Twice named an "All-American City." Two hundred square miles, 323,000 people, a dozen competing and overlapping governmental units, resegregating schools. Harbison, the Doxiadis Study, the equal employment plan, a two-party system. New industrial plants in the suburban outer reaches. The broad avenues. A major university in the heart of downtown.

Under a benevolent April sun, squirrels play chase around the live oaks beside the State House. The azaleas are glorious. In the distance, a bell chimes softly.

Time, for the South, is reduced to *now*. One generation. Twenty years.

Culture: Reexploring "The Sahara of the Bozart"

In the style and spirit of the times in which he wrote, Henry Louis Mencken was a perfect embodiment of personal journalism, a slashing and fearless critic of all things sacred and profane. His prejudices were like a sailor's tattoos—visible, irreverent, outrageous. He was a master of invective, a person of deep intellect and insight, a man of wit and humor and cynicism—in short, an immensely talented and colorful and complex character.

Near the mid-point of his career, he wrote a six-volume series of essays which he called, with characteristic bluntness, *Prejudices,* and in the second volume, which came out in 1920, there was an essay called "The Sahara of the Bozart." Its subject was the South as a cultural wasteland, and it is hard to imagine a criticism more unsparingly acerbic and devastating. It was a hatchet job of the first order—made the more unbear-

able to Southerners, no doubt, because its excesses were inter-
larded with so much truth.

The South, he wrote, is so large that "nearly the whole of
Europe could be lost in that stupendous region of fat farms,
shoddy cities and paralyzed cerebrums," and yet "for all its
size and all its wealth and all the 'progress' it babbles of, it is
almost as sterile, artistically, intellectually, culturally, as the
Sahara Desert. There are single acres in Europe that house
more first-rate men than all the states south of the Potomac."
Indeed, he wrote, it is "amazing to contemplate so vast a
vacuity," and it would be "impossible in all history to match
so complete a drying-up of a civilization."

Before the Civil War, said Mencken, the South produced
"superior men" with "active and original minds"; they were
"hospitable and tolerant," they had "the vague thing that we
call culture." But not in 1920: "In all that gargantuan paradise of the fourth-rate there is not a single picture gallery
worth going into, or a single orchestra capable of playing the
nine symphonies of Beethoven, or a single opera-house, or a
single theatre devoted to decent plays, or a single public
monument . . . that is worth looking at, or a single workshop
devoted to the making of beautiful things." With only a couple
of exceptions, he went on, there were no poets "above the rank
of neighborhood rhymester" and no prose writers "who can
actually write," and as for critics, composers, painters, sculp-
tors, architects, historians, sociologists, philosophers, theologians, and scientists, "there is not even a bad one between the
Potomac mud-flats and the Gulf."

Mencken called Virginia "the most civilized of southern
states, now as always," but he found little there to cheer him:
Her politics "are cheap, ignorant, parochial, idiotic . . . a
Washington or a Jefferson, dumped there by some act of God,
would be denounced as a scoundrel and jailed overnight." And
if Virginia "is the best of the south to-day," then Georgia "is
perhaps the worst. The one is simply senile; the other is crass,

gross, vulgar and obnoxious. Between lies a vast plain of mediocrity, stupidity, lethargy, almost of dead silence. In the north, of course, there is also grossness, crassness, vulgarity. The north, in its way, is also stupid and obnoxious. But nowhere in the north is there such complete sterility, so depressing a lack of all civilized gesture and aspiration."

Having thus warmed up to his subject, Mencken went on for almost twenty pages. Near the end he asserted that

it is impossible for intelligence to flourish in such an atmosphere. Free inquiry is blocked by the idiotic certainties of ignorant men. The arts, save in the lower reaches of the gospel hymn, the phonograph and the chautauqua harangue, are all held in suspicion. The tone of public opinion is set by an upstart class but lately emerged from industrial slavery into commercial enterprise—the class of "hustling" business men, of "live wires," of commercial club luminaries, of "drive" managers, of forward-lookers and right-thinkers—in brief, of third-rate southerners inoculated with all the worst traits of the Yankee sharper. . . . The southerner, at his worst, is never quite the surly cad that the Yankee is. His sensitiveness may betray him into occasional bad manners, but in the main he is a pleasant fellow—hospitable, polite, good-humored, even jovial. . . . But a bit absurd. . . . A bit pathetic.

Even the most charitable of Southerners must have found such an overdose of verbal vituperation difficult to swallow. The essay is not an outstanding example of Mencken's consummate journalistic skill—it is, in fact, not journalism but cutthroat criticism—but it does illustrate vividly his power to outrage, and part of that power derived from the incapacity of his victims to make an adequate defense against his outpourings of abuse. In point of fact, the South in 1920 did not have much to boast of in the fields of art, music, theater, literature, and the academic disciplines—it was not as barren as Mencken pictured it, but it offered a uniformly unfavorable comparison with other regions of the country. Mencken was looking for what he called in his essay "American *Kultur*"—by which he meant, presumably, the formal manifestations of what was good and true and beautiful. He did not say whose definitions of goodness and truth and beauty should be applied—his own, presumably, or those of some other "higher authority"—but clearly almost nothing he saw in the South satisfied him, and it must have been painful for irate Southerners to have so little to offer in rebuttal.

Had he been around to take another look fifty years later, Mencken no doubt would have been compelled to acknowledge some remarkable changes. There are art galleries and symphony orchestras and theaters of impressive quality in the South now, and there are poets and fiction writers and composers and artists and academicians of national renown. The Sahara, irrigated by indigenous and upcountry fountains, has bloomed and flowered a bit in the past half-century.

It might be of some passing interest to tote up all the blossoms and attempt some quantitative and qualitative comparisons with other regions. But that has already been done very ably by Roger Griffin Hall in a chapter of *You Can't Eat Magnolias,* and in any event, H. L. Mencken's concept of culture (and Hall's) draws too tight a circle to encompass all that belongs in a broader definition, such as Webster's: "the habits, skills, arts, instruments, institutions, etc. of a given people in a given period." Leaving aside the elements of "high culture," there is much in the music, religion, communication arts, life styles, and leisure-time habits of Southerners—and Americans generally—that helps to define them. The manners, tastes, emotions, customs, traditions, social conventions, interests, values, mores, morals, beliefs, proficiencies, and priorities of Americans in the 1970s—in short, the things people devote their time and energy and money to, aside from the basic necessities of life—amount to far more than orchestras and art galleries and academic pursuits, however important those things may be.

In that larger context, the South is certainly not a cultural wasteland. For good and ill, it resembles the rest of America more and more with each passing year. There is developing an increasingly dominant and singular American culture, overlaying myriads of subcultures that struggle constantly for their identity and survival. The subcultures are like the people who comprise them—new ones are born of purposeful union or accidental conjugation, old ones die of neglect or old age. Any examination of elements of the larger culture, or of some of the smaller ones, is apt to show how powerful the process of Americanization has become—and Southern contributions to that process are by no means lacking. Whether or not one approves of these trends, they exist. A caravan crossing Mencken's Sahara in the 1970s can send out picture postcards that will amaze and delight and confuse and disturb and infuriate natives and outlanders alike.

Hemingway Stadium on the campus of the University of Mississippi in Oxford is one of the holy temples of the American Way of Life. On Saturday afternoons in the rust and amber glow of autumn, the religion of the masses is celebrated there with all the ritual and pageantry and spectacle of a High Church ceremony. The sacraments of the faith, the symbols that constitute the religion itself, are paraded before the assembled multitude, and each one is accorded the highest measure of respect.

There is, to begin, Patriotism, symbolized by the waving banners of Mississippi, the Old Confederacy, and the United States, and by the playing of "Dixie" and the National Anthem. There is Militarism, personified by an ROTC honor guard, and perhaps by a visiting astronaut or a returned ex-prisoner of war. There is Prayer ("May we all be winners in the Game of Life, in Jesus' name we pray, amen"). There is Music, live and in color, performed with skill and precision by the marching bands. There is Conspicuous Consumption—all tickets of admission to the temple are $7 apiece, and most of the 37,500 people there are on a three-day weekend pilgrimage that will cost far more, even seventy times seven. There is Politics, in the person of important public officials and other influential Mississippians, guests of the university president, who sit in special boxes on the 50-yard line. There is Sex: beautiful young cheerleaders and majorettes showing lots of pink flesh, coeds and older women in the crowd dressed to the eyelashes in all the latest fashions. There is White Supremacy, no longer regulated by law but by economics and custom and tradition: the overwhelming whiteness of the crowd, the teams, the coaches, the press, the referees, and the ancient gestures that evoke an unforgotten past—Rebel yells, the waving of the Stars and Bars. And finally, there is Sport—the game itself, the main attraction, the warfare, the applied science of organized violence.

Hemingway Stadium, it should be quickly added, is not the only holy temple, nor is Ole Miss by any means the only keeper of the faith. In fact, the presence of more football coaches than English professors and a long tradition of allowing the athletic tail to wag its academic dog have not been enough to keep the University of Mississippi at the pinnacle of intercollegiate sports. As football has risen to the status of a national folk religion, Southern colleges and universities have been taking it on the chin from the likes of UCLA, Nebraska, Oklahoma, Southern California, and Ohio State. The newest weapon in the arsenal of the gladiators is the black superstar, and the South, being a little late in getting the message, has fallen behind. So it is not the Mississippi, or the Southern, but the *American* Way of Life that is being celebrated in the coliseums of the land; leave aside the symbols of white supremacy (and they *are* being left aside, with accelerating swiftness, by Southern institutions), and the rest of the pomp and ceremony can be witnessed in hundreds of stadiums across the nation.

Athletics may be doing as much to influence racial attitudes in the United States as the emergence of economic and political black power. The desegregation of higher education, in and out of the South, had been led by the black athlete, and blacks have excelled to such an extent that they very nearly dominate the basketball courts and are more than holding their own on the football fields. Segregation, as powerful as it once was, could not forever stand in the way of a conference title or a bowl bid or a spot in the national rankings, and even the most racist fans now appear to accept, however cheerfully, the lofty status of black heroes as well as white ones. So the Confederate flags are being furled, and the strains of "Dixie" are fading, and not all of the female flesh is pink, and not all of the muscular he-men are blue-eyed blonds, and the South is rising again to athletic prominence.

Notwithstanding the alleged virtues of big-time college athletics—school spirit, sportsmanship, character building, national recognition, and all the rest—there is an unsavory side as well. Intense competition and pressure lead to recruiting violations, manipulation of admissions requirements, cheating in the academic realm, increased violence on the field, and the spread of gambling. The exploitation of athletes has also become a widespread problem, and black athletes in particular appear to have been most affected. "College athletics have grown into a billion-dollar industry, and no one in power wants to let go," wrote the New York *Times*'s veteran sports columnist Arthur Daley in the spring of 1973. "The one simple solution is to stop buying athletes and to use students instead of mercenaries. But since this would mean a return to the horse-and-buggy days, it is manifestly impossible. So college athletics go careening down the road at a breakneck pace, headed for an inevitable crack-up."

The expansion of professional sports and the influence of television on athletics have greatly altered the nature of college competition; what was once legitimately sport is now entertainment, spectacle, and big business, beyond the control of coaches and professors and presidents and susceptible to the influences of corporate and entrepreneurial executives, lawyers, government officials, and gamblers. And since 1960, when Dallas and Houston landed major-league franchises in professional football, pro sports have spread to half a dozen Southern cities. There is as much pennant fever and Super Bowl hysteria in Atlanta and New Orleans and Miami now as there is in Pittsburgh or Los Angeles or Green Bay, Wisconsin.

Sports fanaticism is not a new phenomenon on the American scene, nor is it altogether unhealthy. But the degree of pressure and preoccupation and saturation has risen in the past decade, in parallel with such other developments as the spread of television, the rise in affluence, and the advance of desegregation. There is a seemingly insatiable appetite for fantasy and diversion and high adventure vicariously enjoyed, and the sports extravaganza brings it all together for spectators, whether they are part of the throng on the scene or among the millions who watch the tube.

The ritual that is acted out now with such devotion and seriousness in the nation's stadiums may say as much about the culture and the character of Americans as events in the Colosseum revealed about the Romans nineteen centuries ago. The fascination with violence, the effects of mob psychology, the exhilaration of victory, the element of voyeurism, the sense of liberation from inhibitions, the desire to excel and conquer, the hint of decadence—all are part of the experience encompassed by big-time sports, and that experience is an all-American affair. And if there is legitimacy to the comparison between Romans and Americans, then President Nixon, the nation's number one sports fan, is a modern Nero, having elevated athletics to a level of importance no element of high culture can come close to matching. Nixon may even owe a large measure of his electoral success to his devotion to sports; as a master politician, he could not have failed to notice that University of Texas football coach Darrell Royal is as well known in his state as John Connally, or that George Wallace is no less revered in his home state than the University of Alabama's football coach, Paul "Bear" Bryant.

Football is not the only sport enjoying national popularity. Major-league professional baseball, basketball, golf, and even ice hockey have spread from the North and East through the West and South, drawing large crowds and generating a massive turnover of cash. Automobile racing, once limited mainly to an annual event in Indianapolis, now attracts thousands of devoted followers to tracks all over the country, and Southern stock-car drivers have roared off the backcountry dirt tracks onto the hard-surface ovals to win prominence and prosperity in the sport. Stock-car racing, in fact, is dominated by Southern drivers; it is the best current example of a Southern sport gone national, in contrast to the national sports that have been moving into the South.

One interesting consequence of the elevation of sports in national life has been the emergence of the millionaire athlete. In virtually every sport there are proliferating numbers of men (but not women) whose earnings have put them in a class with corporation executives and businessmen and entertainers and political giants. Many of them are not just rich; they are also national celebrities, heroes who enjoy the adulation of the masses. Horatio Alger stories are as common as athlete's foot among them—every schoolboy knows about the rags-to-riches rise of superstars such as Joe Namath, Willie Mays, Wilt Chamberlain, and Lee Trevino. A story from South Carolina in the fall of 1972 seemed more Algerian than the great Horatio himself could have created. It was written by Jack Bass of the Charlotte *Observer*. Here are parts of it:

YEMASSEE, S.C.—Nick Zeigler interrupted his campaign for the U.S. Senate Tuesday to attend a small candlelight dinner hosted by the new master of Brewton Plantation.

The 368-acre plantation dates back 240 years to a royal grant from King George II of England, and one of the early owners was Charles Pinckney, a signer of the Constitution. George Washington paid a visit there in 1791.

The new owner is Joe Frazier, heavyweight boxing champion of the world and a man whose ancestors were slaves at similar plantations elsewhere in his native Beaufort County.

"He's a delightful person," Zeigler said of Frazier after the dinner, which featured both soul food and wine served by black attendants wearing white jackets.

Zeigler [noted the] "very human story" of Frazier's rise from the 13th child of a poor black family . . . to the owner of a plantation he bought as a place for his mother to live. Zeigler's ancestors were plantation owners and slaveholders before the Civil War.

It takes a little of the edge off the story—but only a little—to note that Frazier subsequently lost his heavyweight crown to another fast riser, George Foreman, and Zeigler lost his bid for the Senate to incumbent superseg J. Strom Thurmond. Frazier and his arch-foe in the ring, Muhammad Ali, have both been toppled from boxing's mountaintop, but neither of them has been cast back into poverty—and Frazier's sixty-five-year-old mother is still living in the white-columned plantation house that had to be rebuilt more than a hundred years ago after it was burned by General Sherman's troops during the Civil War.

One other story from the world of sports should be mentioned. It was in the newspapers in May 1973, and it is self-explanatory:

Hank Aaron, the Atlanta Braves' super slugger who is fast approaching Babe Ruth's career record of 714 home runs, says he receives hate mail every day berating him because he is a black man approaching a white man's record.

"Last week I got 416 pieces of mail one day and 600-some-odd the next," the 39-year-old star said. "I'd say that 60 percent of it is of a racist nature.

"If I were a white man, all America would be proud of me. But I'm black. You have to be black in America to know how sick some people are."

The changing life styles of Americans—not just sports heroes but all kinds of people—is a development that reflects both disenchantment with the dominant culture and a fascination with elements of a variety of subcultures. Unprecedented affluence still beckons the majority to the Good Life, and their expenditures for material comforts—cars, boats, appliances, vacation homes—reach new record highs each year, but against that trend the rising consciousness of groups of people coalescing around racial, ethnic, religious, economic, sexual, chronological, or political affinity is very much in evidence. Black Americans, who number almost 25 million and who are in themselves a richly varied group, have had a profound influence on the language, fashions, music, and entertainment tastes of Americans generally, and the assertions of black identity, consciousness, power, nationalism, pride, and solidarity have spawned similar assertions by others, from Indians and Puerto Ricans and Chicanos and white ethnics and mountaineers to women and young people and the elderly.

Yet for all that, the drawing power of the American middle class remains the dominant force. Its capacity for coopting and assimilating tributary movements into the main current of society is both inspiring and frightening—inspiring because of its potential for creating an open and diverse society, and frightening because of its tendency to produce homogenization and conformity. The groups and individuals who pursue life styles that deviate from the cultural mainstream find it more and more difficult to sustain their individuality, whether their aim is radical revolution or benevolent nonconformity.

In its latter-day yearning for equal status in the Union, the South has exhibited a willingness to adopt uncritically the trappings of the dominant culture, and to be intolerant of people who diverge conspicuously from that course. Conformity has long been a tradition in the South, and that tradition persists now, even though there has been a substantial change in the things to which people are expected to conform. Subcultural and countercultural movements and alternative life styles have been visible in the South in recent years, of course, as they have been all over the United States, but they have not thrived there; in fact, the South may be leading the trend toward national cultural homogenization.

If that is so, then the odyssey of Chess McCartney is all the more remarkable. For thirty-five years, McCartney has devoted himself in solitude to a way of life that is the very antithesis of materialism and affluence and upward mobility, and he has stayed at it in spite of ridicule and rejection and abuse.

Born and raised on an Iowa farm, he saw his livelihood washed away by the Depression, and he worked for the WPA until he was crippled by an accident on the job. When he was able to walk—but unable to work—he decided to hit the road with a wagon and a team of goats, and he subsequently traveled well over 100,000 miles through forty-nine states in that unorthodox fashion, using a small plot of land near Jeffersonville, Georgia, as his home base.

The last time I saw McCartney was in the summer of 1971. He had pulled his wagon off the shoulder of U.S. Highway 41 a few miles north of Marietta, Georgia, and stopped it on a gentle slope under some trees. Dusk was approaching, and the goats were tethered and grazing among the weeds, and Chess had a little fire going.

Rushing past with all the other absent-minded motorists, I almost didn't see him, but I turned around at the first opportunity and went back. He hardly looked up when my sons and I got out of the car. To him, I was just one more curious fellow traveler eager to ply him with questions—one too many after a long day on the road. But to me, he was like an apparition from the past.

The first and only time I had ever seen the Goat Man before was on a summer evening in the early 1940s, when he was camped for the night on a river bank just outside the little Kentucky town where I lived. I must have been about eight at the time, and I remember standing watchfully with some of my buddies at a respectful distance from the wagon and the goats.

We talked about it for days afterward, about that mysterious and wonderful man with the bushy hair and the long beard and the eyes that had a magician's glint in them, and we day-dreamed about tying some clothes on a stick and joining him out there on the open road.

And now I was a middle-aged, middle-class journeyman on another road, and there was old Chess, pushing seventy-five, still on his pilgrimage and looking just the way I remembered him back when I was a kid and life was just a bowl of cherries. I watched my sons gaze in awe and wonderment at the eighteen goats and the ramshackle wagon with its iron wheels and its tin roof and its tiny sleeping compartment and its assortment of tied-on paraphernalia and its PREPARE TO MEET THY GOD sign on top, and I saw a reflection of myself on their faces.

He sold me some postcards picturing himself and his wagon team—the cards are his principal means of income—and a little booklet called "Who the Goat Man Is." In it, he had written:

I have been called crazy, stupid, ignorant, and many other uncomplimentary names because of my way of life—herding a passel of smelly goats from Florida to Maine to Washington and California. The goats have taught me a lot in the past 30 years. They don't, for example, care how I smell or how I look. They trust me and have faith in me, and this is more than I can say about a lot of people. During my years on the road I have been reviled, cursed, beaten and shot at. I have been denied access to public accommodations, but I have survived. I am an ordained preacher, and I try my best with my limited education to explain God's work to the people. I see a lot of race hate during my travels, both in the South and in the North. And I can see more of it coming. It will end only when Christ returns to Earth, and I predict that this will be soon. I feel though that preaching about the second coming of Christ is a bit foolish, for too many people haven't yet heard about the first coming.

His supper was ready, and it was time for us to leave. As we started for the car, he pulled one more postcard from the wagon and handed it to me. "You can have this," he said, with the slightest trace of a smile. "One of the goats autographed it." It was a large card with a color photograph of the bib-overalled Goat Man, Bible in hand, standing in a cotton patch. A corner of the card had been bitten off.

No one, least of all Chess McCartney, would suggest that driving a team of goats around America is a viable and attractive alternative life style for people who are disenchanted with the values and the strictures of middle-class society, nor could it be argued convincingly that McCartney has made a valuable contribution to the culture. But his long and solitary journey belongs to a tradition that is as old as the road itself, and it deserves to be remembered. Like the gypsies and the hoboes and the vagabonds, he was one of the early Easy Riders, a forerunner of the beatniks and the hippies and the Jesus freaks. His life as a wanderer may say less about him than it says about the rest of us, for it raises a disturbing question: What is it about life in this country that makes thousands of young people—the spiritual heirs of Chess McCartney—take to the open road?

So there ought to be a monument to the Goat Man in Jeffersonville, Georgia, or somewhere else along the way, and the inscription on it might say something like this: "Chess McCartney, the Goat Man, spent thirty-five years on the road, searching for America. He stayed at it longer than a lot of famous men, including John Gunther, John Steinbeck, Woody Guthrie, Jack Kerouac, Bill Moyers, and Charles Kuralt, and he also outlasted a far larger number who were not so famous. Like all of them, he never found it. Like only a few, he never stopped looking."

This generation's new seekers don't last long as loners. They gravitate to the communes and the cooperatives and the collectives, and still the attrition rate among them is high. The cities of the South—Atlanta, New Orleans, Miami—have had their colonies of transient young people, their drug scene, their counterculture, their waves of runaway teenagers, their young religionists, the same as cities elsewhere have had. In the South as in other places, the rural communes seem less plagued by impermanence than the urban ones, perhaps because they have the advantage of a little land and open space, and at least the potential of a degree of self-sufficiency.

One of the oldest—aside from such religious groups as the Mormons, the Amish, and the Mennonites—is Koinonia Farm near Americus, Georgia. It was started in 1942 by Clarence Jordan, a Southern Baptist minister who wanted to build "an integrated, Christian community" in the heart of the south Georgia black belt. Koinonia survived the threats and violence of white law officers and vigilante groups, grand jury charges of communism, Ku Klux Klan terrorism, and the hostility of the white church, and when Jordan died a few years ago his community was larger than ever and firmly established in a program of home building, farming, and economic development. Incorporated as Koinonia Partners, its goals are to "emancipate" land for low-income farm families to work together in partnership, to create low-overhead, rural-based industries for job opportunity, and to offer no-interest loans to poor families who want to own their own homes. Quoting St. Augustine ("He who possesses a surplus possesses the goods of others"), Jordan used to assert: "That is a polite way of saying that anybody who has too much is a thief. If you are a 'thief,' perhaps you should set a reasonable living standard for your family and restore the 'stolen goods' to humanity through some suitable means."

If that was enough to put conventional churchmen and anticommunist zealots in an orbit of outrage, it was also enough to attract a lot of poor families, white as well as black, and it brought in such people as a wandering prophet named Ashton Jones and a young millionaire named Millard Fuller and a rich assortment of others who understood and accepted Jordan's radical theology. Dallas Lee has written a good account of Clarence Jordan and the Koinonia story in his book *The Cotton Patch Evidence*. As for Jordan himself, his legacy would be rich enough if it were nothing else than the spirit that permeates Koinonia, but there is more: His "Cotton Patch Version" of the New Testament, a modern translation with a Southern accent, is a theological gift to the people he loved—which is to say people everywhere—and while it may make scholars shudder and strict constructionists cringe, it also breathes humor and earthiness and vitality into the ancient words of the Bible. Paul's Epistles to the Romans, the Corinthians, the Ephesians, the Thessalonians, and the Philippians become letters to the Christians in Washington, Atlanta, Birmingham, Selma, and the Alabaster African Church in Smithville, Alabama. A quotation from Matthew 1:18 gives a hint of the tone and flavor:

The beginning of Jesus the Leader was like this: While his mama, Mary, was engaged to Joseph, but before they had relations, she was made pregnant by the Holy Spirit. Since Joseph, her fiancé, was a considerate man and didn't want to make a public scandal, he decided to quietly break up with her. As he was wondering about the whole situation, a messenger from the Lord came to him in a dream and said, "Joe Davidson, don't be ashamed to marry Mary, because the Holy Spirit has made her pregnant. Now she'll give birth to a boy, who you'll name Jesus, because he will deliver his nation from their errors."

The Cotton Patch Version is no mere parody; it is a painstaking translation of most of the New Testament into the vernacular of the rural South, and as such it is a valuable addition to the culture—not just of the South, but of the nation.

Clarence Jordan was a unique character, and he left an unmistakable imprint with his translation and with Koinonia. There is only one Cotton Patch Version, but there are many communal and cooperative enterprises similar to Koinonia in almost every Southern state, and there is an indigenous Southerness about them that is not found elsewhere. The Highlander Research and Education Center near New Market, in the mountains of Tennessee, is one example, and Providence Farm near Tchula, Mississippi, is another. The Southwest Georgia Project, near Albany, has developed under the able leadership of former SNCC leader Charles Sherrod, and Penn Community Services, in the coastal island region of South Carolina, has been serving the black community of that area since 1862, when it was established as the first school in the South for freed slaves. Under the guidance of John Gadson and Freida Mitchell, Penn has expanded its program to include land reform, housing and economic development, early childhood education, and cultural enrichment.

Each of these cooperative ventures and the others like them are examples of the continuing search for workable alternatives to a dominant culture that has often been inhospitable, oppressive, and repugnant to people it perceived as "different." Another type of communal enterprise, starkly contrasting with these but far more typical of the collectives young people have been forming in recent years, has taken roots near the village of Summertown, Tennessee. It is called The Farm, and its similarities and dissimilarities to places like Koinonia and Penn make an interesting study.

The Farm is a "family monastery" of over 600 adults and children who live on more than 1,500 acres of woods and fields under the watchful eye of a college professor-turned-guru named Stephen Gaskin. It is a commune of like-minded young people who get their spiritual sustenance from Oriental mysticism, Western religions, nature, marijuana, and Gaskin—especially Gaskin. With allowances for some qualification and at the risk of oversimplifying, it is possible to say generally what they are for and what they are against: They are for love, peace, marriage (including group marriage, in multiples of two), cohabitation, nature, organic foods, marijuana, peyote, rock music (some of it), communication, reality, sorghum molasses, soybeans, midwives, education (through the eighth grade), compassion, honesty, manual labor, technology (some of it), and their neighbors. They are against meat, dairy products, fish, poultry, eggs, cheese, birth control, abortion, pornography, materialism, pop art, acid and all chemical drugs, alcohol, tobacco, heroin, political activism, fighting, greed, and "square hairs" (long-haired kids who get into hassles with the police).

Many members of the commune were among several hundred young people who left San Francisco with Gaskin in 1970 in a caravan in search of a rural settling place. The Summertown farm eventually turned out to be the place they were looking for, and they have thrived there, in spite of some setbacks. In 1971, Gaskin and three others were arrested for growing marijuana; their subsequent convictions and one-to-three-year sentences are under appeal on the constitutional ground that the use of the drug is essential to their free exercise of religion. After they got over the shock of seeing so many "long-haired hippie freaks," The Farm's neighbors around Summertown and Lewis County seemed to get used to the idea, and the gentle and unaggressive communards have come to be regarded with tolerance.

The Farm community is made up primarily of white, middle-class casualties of the Affluent Society, young people who dropped out of the rat race but couldn't buy the violence-and-revolution philosophy that so fascinated one wing of the counterculture. Most of them were looking for a spiritual leader who could give them an alternative to the ways of living that had brought them such confusion and alienation and grief, and in Gaskin they found him.

Gaskin is a frail, stoop-shouldered man in his mid-thirties whom one of his admirers once described as "a human energy so powerful that it rushes through your being like a wild wind! You are destroyed, but not hurt. Instead you are magically transformed with him into one great vibration of Joy—all beautiful and bejeweled in the act of touching and knowing . . . the Truth, the Real, the One." That's heavy stuff, and to his near-sycophantic disciples he is a heavy dude. In the commune, he is a benevolent dictator—the rulemaker, teacher, high priest, and judge of last resort—and from every indication, he is all of those things by unanimous and eager acclaim. So much adulation inevitably affects him, and he is given on occasion to considerations of immortality, as in this exchange with a questioner at an off-the-farm appearance:

Question: Does God speak through you?
Gaskin: Sometimes.
Question: Are you a messiah?
Gaskin: I don't know. I ain't done yet. It never hurts to try. You'll have to wait until I'm gone before that can be answered.
Question: What is your long-range goal?
Gaskin: I'm out to save the world.
Question: How?
Gaskin: I don't know yet. I ain't done.

Back when he was teaching creative writing and semantics at San Francisco State College and lecturing among the multitudes in his "Monday Night Class" at a place called the Family Dog, he wrote an article for *Motive* magazine in which he described how he used his "LSD-sharpened perceptions to steer the class into higher vibrational ranges. There is chanting, lecturing and questions and answers on such topics as what to do when stoned, how to make love, what to do about the draft, how to manifest a groovy trip, 'Who is God?' . . ." He added: "Much of the psychic technology we use is in the form of aphorisms learned 'on the hoof' while on LSD." Among the aphorisms: "We are all one." "You can't go anywhere that you can't get back from." "Everyone creates everything that happens to him." "God is love." Although the words of wisdom may seem austere, he wrote, "when it comes to the actual practice, the prime instruction is stay loose, groovy, high, happy and compassionate, to manifest the kingdom here and now, with or without the assistance of drugs."

In Summertown, LSD is a no-no. Aside from their cere-
monial uses of pot, which the Lewis County sheriff now says he
won't interefere with, the commune members profess to be no
longer interested in drugs. They are busy growing crops and
building houses. They have formed a nonprofit corporation
which has an annual budget of about $250,000, and while their
farm products, Gaskin's published writings, their contracted
labor for others, and a record their traveling rock band has
made bring in some income, the bulk of it comes from the
members' contributions of savings, stocks, property, and in-
heritances. They publish an annual report, including a financial statement.

In many ways, the members of The Farm bear a physical
and spiritual resemblance to the Mennonite colony that has
long lived nearby. The Gaskinites are said by their neighbors
to "have a good name," and be "honest to a fault." Their long
hair and beards, their bib overalls and granny dresses and sun
bonnets, give them an anachronistic appearance, like nineteenth-century frontier people. They are friendly, generous,
peaceful, hard-working, law-abiding and—in their own distinctive manner—pious, moralistic, and orthodox. In fact, what is
most astonishing about them after a while is just that ortho-
doxy, a fundamental conservatism of philosophy and outlook
that is the very opposite of the sort of radicalism that has
commonly (and inaccurately) been ascribed to almost every
movement in the countercultures of the young.

The Summertown commune is vastly different from the
Southern cooperative ventures described or mentioned in passing earlier. At places like Koinonia the preoccupations, out of
necessity, have revolved around such issues as race, poverty,
cultural identity, economic survival, and political unity, and
their religious faith often has propelled them into the struggle.
The Gaskinites, on the other hand, have had no appreciable
involvement in any of those issues, and their spiritual activity
has led in the direction of withdrawal rather than engagement.

The Farm has far more in common with the colonies of

young people that have been sprinkled across the West in an arc from Colorado and New Mexico up to Oregon and Washington. Like most of them, it is made up principally of refugees from suburban splendor, young immigrants who have renounced the materialism (but not always the money) of their fathers and gone in search of a utopia where life can be simple again, the way it is thought to have been once upon a time. They are mixing a heady potion of idealism and innocence and determination and naïveté and human frailty, and nobody really knows yet what that chemistry will produce. But experiments in group living and pilgrimages to greener pastures and quests for new life styles have been going on since Eden, and utopia still eludes its pursuers like a mirage, and it is hard to imagine that this time will be different. Will The Farm last as long as the Mormons? The Amish? The Mennonites? Koinonia? Chess McCartney? Not even a guru like Stephen Gaskin has the answer. To paraphrase him, they ain't done yet.

Closer to the mainstream, the Jesus freaks have occupied a sort of way station between the mysticism of drug-oriented communes and the materialism of establishment-oriented churches. The South was an especially fertile breeding ground for their brand of fundamentalism, and thousands of young people on the way back up from the drug trip stopped off at the smaller, city-based communes where born-again former hippies and teenie boppers were getting high on Jesus.

Some of those places still exist, but most have either broken up or moved closer to the conventional churches (modifying them in the process) and closer to the crowded right flank of the American religious experience.

Waiting for them there, just outside the doors of the multitude of conservative denominations, were such groups as the Campus Crusade for Christ and the Fellowship of Christian Athletes, and such magnetic evangelical figures as Billy Gra-

ham and Oral Roberts. In June of 1972, the Campus Crusade
for Christ and its guiding light, a California industrialist
named Bill Bright, staged the International Student Congress
on Evangelism in the Cotton Bowl in Dallas, and some 80,000
delegates from all fifty states and sixty foreign countries
showed up, prompting Graham to call it a "religious Wood-
stock . . . the greatest religious happening in history."

Most of the participants in Explo '72, as the event was
commonly called, were white, middle-class young people. They
were served spellbinding sermons by Graham, who told them
long hair and beards were okay with God, as long as they
stayed clean in mind and body; pep talks by athletes, including Dallas Cowboy quarterback Roger Staubach, who told
them "God has given us good field position" in the game of
life; amplified music by rock groups in far-out costumes on
psychedelic sets, groups like the Armageddon Experience and
the Jesus Sound Explosion; and country-pop songs with a
spiritual flavor by Johnny Cash and Kris Kristofferson. The
response throughout the week-long revival was thunderous
applause, reverberating cheers, and a sea of upraised index
fingers, signifying that Jesus was Number One.

The basic objective of Explo '72 was scaled to the dimensions of Graham's rhetoric: it was to lay the groundwork for an
evangelistic juggernaut that would convert the nation to Jesus
Christ by 1976 and the whole world by 1980. The most sophisticated methods of the corporate enterprise, from computer
technology and mass communications to the newest techniques
of salesmanship, were employed in the training sessions. The
delegates paid a $25 registration fee and $50 for room and
board, and most of them apparently would have given ten
times that much for the experience. The 2,000 or so blacks in
attendance seemed equally as taken by it all as their white
brothers and sisters.

J. Claude Evans, the chaplain of Southern Methodist University, wrote an account of the event for the newspaper

American Report, and in it he said: "If Explo is to be faulted, it must be on a deeper level than finances or racial bias." He was critical of its "theological thinness," its slick and over-simplified "how to" techniques, and its "full-blown fundamentalist interpretation of Christianity." The Campus Crusade for Christ, he wrote, "would be more honest if it admitted, both to itself and to the public, that it is really a church denomination of its own."

Whatever it is, the CCC pulled a real coup in Dallas. In one stroke, it probably did more to coopt the Jesus freaks than Billy Graham himself could do even if he took his personal crusade to every commune in the country. And in any event, separating Graham from the CCC would be as difficult as separating him from the Southern Baptists, or the White House, or the television camera. He has long since risen above Baptism and his North Carolina roots to become the nation's unofficial chaplain and a globetrotting messenger of the Lord.

Graham has changed a lot in the thirty-five years since God called him on a golf course in Florida and told him to be a minister. His evangelistic enterprise is now a $15-million-a-year business. He calls on kings and popes and presidents, he draws massive audiences wherever he goes, his voice and image are broadcast to millions by radio and television each week. At fifty-four, he is more than ever the handsome, jut-jawed, leonine eminence, God's Golden Boy, a devil-slayer whose sword is his silver tongue. His blond, wavy hair, now streaked with gray and curling fashionably over the collar of his coat, seems a part with his new mod wardrobe.

For more than twenty years, Graham has insisted that his crusades be open to all races and creeds. "Jesus Christ wasn't a white man," he can be heard exclaiming, "and Christianity isn't a white man's religion." Billy is keeping score; he knows what color the world is, and he wants the gospel he proclaims to envelop everybody. He has the instincts of a monopolist, and like the industrial and political and military monopolists of his time, he understands the relationships of numbers and growth and power. He has taken the old-time religion of his native South out into the nation and the world, leaving in his wake such lesser evangelists as Bob Jones and Carl McIntyre, whose ultraconservative approach has been to rail against blacks and Catholics and Jews and Moslems, while Graham's more astute strategy has been to try to convert them.

Graham has identified himself with moderate racial change and with such events as Explo '72 in such a way as to stay in the forefront of the American religious scene. In doing so, he has firmly established himself as the single most influential figure in what can fairly be called the Southernization of American religion, for in spite of his moderate views on race— views the Protestant South does not fully share even yet—virtually everything else he stands for is straight out of the history and traditions of Southern Protestantism.

The Southern Baptist Convention, whose 12 million members make it the largest Protestant denomination in the world, is Billy Graham's mother church, but like Jesus, Graham is too deeply engaged in larger affairs to spend all his time with his mother. "I am a member of the world church first," he says, "and of the Southern Baptist Convention second." Even without full claim to him, though, the SBC has moved beyond the borders of the South, expanding rapidly in the North and West, riding the crest of a conservative wave that is packing the churches that incline in the direction of fundamentalism and emptying the ones that tend to be classified as liberal.

There are at least twenty-five different Baptist bodies in the United States, with an aggregate membership of more than 25 million, and there may be as many as 15 million additional conservative Protestants in a host of denominations who share many of the same theological views. The essential difference between Billy Graham and those institutions is that the institutions cannot envision overcoming their differences to unite under one banner, while Graham can dream of winning them all to the Christ he serves. He is, in a sense, an apostle of conservative ecumenicity. Without the encumbrances of a denominational establishment, he is free to cross the lines of bureaucracy and structure in search of new soldiers for the Lord.

The Southern Baptist Convention and the other Protestant bodies can't do that. At its roots, the SBC is dominated by a strain of conservatism that is not inconsistent with Graham's preachings—it leans to biblical literalism, avoidance of social issues, obedience to authority in the church (but not necessarily in the denomination), personal salvation, patriotism, and proselyting—but the denomination is a bricks-and-mortar institution, and it can't match the maneuverability of a one-man institution like Graham. The SBC, for example, is still racially segregated, in the main, in spite of some efforts in its seminaries, its Christian Life Commission, its urban congregations, and its ranks of young people to change the complexion. Fewer than 1,000 of the denomination's 35,000 churches have even one black member, and the Christian Life Commission, its "conscience watcher" and social concerns arm for the past twenty years, stays constantly in hot water for its efforts to involve Southern Baptists in areas of human service that have more to do with life-serving than with soul-saving.

The second most populous Baptist body after the SBC is the National Baptist Convention, which has more than 5 million members and is the largest black church denomination in the country. The NBC is a reminder of some things about race and religion in the United States that many whites tend to forget, if they ever knew them at all. First, it suggests that black American churchgoers are inclined in general to be as theologically conservative as whites. There are numerous black denominations in addition to the NBC, and most of them can be broadly categorized as conservative. And second, the black church in America has probably grown stronger, not weaker, in the face of desegregation in the larger society; it remains the dominant institution in the black community, while other black institutions have been weakened by the spread of a white-dominated version of integration.

The black church, though it remains essentially segregated, is in far less of a moral quandary about that fact than the white church. Segregation, after all, was a white invention; it was not blacks who imposed it on society, who enforced it, who attempted to elevate it to the status of a cardinal principle ordained by God. White Christians, in and out of the South, now face the paradox of inner division over the issue of race, while their black brothers and sisters, whatever their theological persuasions, are at least united by the fact of their survival and endurance against the injustice and evil of imposed segregation. Black Christians have been bound together and sustained by their faith that God is just, and that his justice will ultimately prevail. White Christians, on the other hand, may be disunited by their belief in a just God, for to some of them, justice would be a vindication, and to others it would be a curse.

The Presbyterian Church in the U.S., a Southern body that broke away from its Northern counterpart in a Civil War split that has never been breached, is one of several predominantly white denominations in which internal tension over racial and social and theological issues has existed for a number of years. One of its ministers, H. Louis Patrick of Trinity Presbyterian Church in Charlotte, North Carolina, has written about Southern religion and culture in a letter published by the *Forum for Contemporary History*.

Southern religion, he wrote, is not simply a reflection of the region's cultural values; it is more nearly the other way around: "Religion is what really makes and keeps the South a separate, solid and stable culture." The South, he said, sees itself as "the true remnant of God's elect," and this "sense of divine election is what makes and keeps the South a region that is both distinct and essentially solid. . . . It removes any

troublesome need for repentance, and it makes all change a
temporary concession to the powers of evil. Only those elected
the way the South is elected are free to glorify the past, sanctify
the present and petrify the future." Patrick believes "this
mystique has created a Southern Protestant Church absolutely
unique in this country. It cuts across denominational lines
while at the same time reinforcing the lines of race and class."
Its theology, he says, is based on a "belief in the literal
inerrancy of the Bible," and its individualism and piety offer
"neither an effective way to change society nor any prophetic
critique of it. Instead, religion works hand-in-glove with the
powers-that-be to conceal the true issues between God and
man."

The "New South," asserts Patrick, "does not exist. And as
long as the religion of the Southern Protestant Church remains
what it is, nothing new will be conceived in, or issue from, the
Southern womb." But, he continues, "The South is returning
to the mainstream of the nation's life. More than that, in the
preservation of a stable society . . . the South is leading the
rest of the land." So maybe the nation's newfound interest in
the South, and in its religious and cultural life in particular,
has come about because (quoting Patrick again) "people at
large see in this region the reflection of that status-quo for
which they long. Not too long ago the gospel according to Billy
Graham was strictly a Southern product. . . . Now, that gospel of individual salvation . . . appeals to persons throughout
the land who struggle with the torment of littleness, trying to
gain some sense of instant worth and welcome from an in-
different civilization that is too complex for their coping."

The vessels in which culture is created and transmitted and
homogenized grow and multiply like hothouse tomatoes. Disney World, the Southern version of Disneyland, is predictably
bigger, costlier, and more fantastic than its parent, a monument to gargantuan artificiality, and its imitators sprout every-

where. One of Disney World's neighbors near Orlando, Florida, will be Bible World, a sort of prefabricated New Jerusalem that will feature a walled city, a six-story mosque, museums, shops, acres of parking spaces, an Easter "Passion Week Panorama," and "the only minaret in the Western hemisphere." Fred C. Tallant, president of a land development company with holdings in Georgia and Florida, says Bible World "will be designed for everyone," and its purpose will be to "inform, entertain and inspire." Tallant, who comes from a Baptist family but describes himself as being not particularly religious, says he and a group of religious Atlanta businessmen hope to make a million dollars in profits from Bible World after its first year of operation.

Movies are another medium shaping cultural styles and patterns, and the trends there, reflected in every region of the country, are now dominated by a mixed bag of black films, by hard-core pornography, and by ever more explicit and sophisticated presentations of violence. The moneymakers are films like *The Godfather, A Clockwork Orange, Straw Dogs, Oh, Calcutta!, Shaft, Super Fly,* and *Deep Throat,* and most of them have enjoyed long runs not only in New York and Los Angeles but in the cities of the Midwest and South and even in the small towns of Middle America. In the spirit of free-enterprise capitalism, entrepreneurs with the keenest instincts for moneymaking have stimulated and exploited a thick seam of public fascination with the manifold forms of physical depravity. Sex-and-violence as a spectator sport is now the movie industry's biggest box office attraction.

Television trails the movies in its treatment of sex and violence, but the lag is not always great; it was TV, after all, that brought the Vietnam war into the nation's living rooms, live and in color, and for blood-and-guts violence, that show was hard to match. Television's continuous image has also blurred the line between the real and the make-believe, giving everything—the war, the news, the commercials, the movies, the network shows—an aura of unreality. As the single most widely used instrument for the continuing education of adults —and for the initiation of children into society—television molds the culture and values and life styles of Americans more than any other thing. And that shaping process is more or less the same everywhere, for the ubiquitous TV screen glows in almost every mansion, apartment, cottage, and cotton-field hovel, and its lights and shadows look the same in New York City and Des Moines and Albuquerque and Holly Springs, Mississippi. Johnny Carson and Barbara Walters and Archie Bunker and Bill Cosby and Walter Cronkite and Dean Martin may have as much to do with what people think and feel and covet as Richard Nixon does, or Billy Graham; each in his own way is an imagemaker and culture shaper. Mighty is the power of the tube.

In the competition for people's time and attention, the print media have yielded ground to television. Newspapers are read as much for their ads and comics and sports and TV listings as for their news and editorials, and among magazines, the death of *Life* and *Look* has left *Reader's Digest* and *TV Guide* at the top of the heap, challenged for readership leadership only by *Playboy* and its imitators, by a host of specialty magazines, and by a dreary profusion of cheap pornography. Regional magazines are also popular: there is *Sunset,* a slick and opulent monthly glorifying the selected virtues of the West, and there is *Southern Living,* which in just eight years has attracted almost a million subscribers with its ad-choked smorgasbord of recipes, fashions, decoration and travel plugs, Old South nostalgia, and New South boosterism.

The South's obeisance to provincialism and piety—the mindset that long kept Prohibition in force, blue laws on the books, *Catcher in the Rye* out of the libraries, and New York magazines off the newsstands—is rapidly eroding. *Jesus Christ Superstar* has packed theaters all over the South, and *Hair* is everywhere; the largest work of art ever created by the late and renowned Pablo Picasso—a 100-foot sculpture entitled *Bust of a Woman*—is being erected at the University of South Florida in Tampa; and *Rolling Stone* gathers no moss among its avid following in the South.

The cultural rites of white Anglo-Saxon Protestants still dominate, but you can find Mexican influences all over Texas, African and Afro-American cultural festivals on dozens of college campuses, a Chinese New Year's parade in Nashville, and a Brazilian Carioca Carnival in Miami, where the Spanish-speaking population now numbers a half-million. In the Cajun country of south Louisiana, where French has traditionally been spoken, about 150 Frenchmen are teaching in the schools in a sort of reverse Peace Corps program jointly financed by France and Louisiana to help preserve the region's linguistic heritage. Even Mississippi has relaxed its border guard: a delegation of Soviet Communist party members visiting Greenville in 1972 was so charmed by Southern hospitality that they chose that Mississippi delta community as their favorite American city. "Here we feel absolutely at home," their leader said.

The magnolia curtain that used to shield the South from cultural breezes is pinned back now, and all sorts of once exotic influences are floating in. There is fire and ice and pollution in those winds—Disney World and Bible World and *Super Fly* and *Deep Throat* and *Hair* and Johnny Carson and *Playboy* and *Rolling Stone* and the Metropolitan Opera and Picasso and the Cubans and the Russians and multitudes of others. The diversity is welcome; certainly it is better to have variety, however mixed its quality may be, than to have a closed and conforming society that regards every stranger as an intruder. But exhilaration would be too strong a response to it all. What is happening to mass culture in the South is what is happening nationwide, and if there is diversity in it, there is also an element of sameness, of homogenization, of artificiality and shallowness and transience.

And finally, there is music. In the perpetuation and diffusion of the many strains of Southern culture, no other instrument carries more force and vitality. The South has been the incubator for most of the indigenous elements in the treasury of American music. It produced jazz and blues and all of their derivations; it spawned country-and-western music, bluegrass, gospel, spirituals; it was a source of rock-'n'-roll, and it has contributed its share of pop and folk and contemporary rock. From W. C. Handy and Louis Armstrong and Bessie Smith and dozens of other giants of an earlier time, through Jimmie Rodgers and Roy Acuff and Bill Monroe and Elvis Presley, and proceeding on to a host of people who are today's superstars, the South can probably claim a longer and more varied roster of nationally influential musicians than any other region of the country.

In almost every one of the major styles of music in America, examples can be found of a substantial Southern contribution, if not of Southern origination. Black Americans—Southerners, more often than not—have enriched the nation's musical heritage out of all proportion to their numbers, and they continue to do so, with more recognition and reward now than ever before. Among instrumental musicians, Earl Scruggs has no peer as a genius of the five-string banjo, Chet Atkins is an acknowledged virtuoso of the guitar, and Guy Carawan, a master of the hammer dulcimer and other instruments of mountain music, is a towering but uncelebrated talent. In the realm of classical music, pianist Van Cliburn, a Texan, has an international reputation, and in the opera, no contemporary star is more luminous than Mississippian Leontyne Price. The rock music and soul music that have so captivated the young in the past decade also have had a Southern flavor; Otis Redding and Janis Joplin are both dead now, but James Brown and Isaac Hayes and the Allman Brothers and many more play on.

And country music, Southern to the core, is warmed by the

echoes of ringing applause and ringing cash registers, not only at the Grand Ole Opry in Nashville but on the West coast, the East coast, the vast reaches in between, and even in London and Tokyo. They go for bluegrass, a pure strain of country, at an annual festival in Tokyo's Hibiya Park; at Wembley Stadium in London, the fifth annual International Festival of Country Music in the spring of 1973 drew fans from almost every European and North American country—including a delegation of nearly eighty musicians and music industry representatives from Nashville.

More than 800 American radio stations are devoted exclusively to country music, and another 1,000 program the country sound at least three hours a day. The Country Music Association, a Nashville-based trade organization, held a meeting of its board of directors in New York's Plaza Hotel in April of 1973, and a few days before that, when country stars Tammy Wynette and George Jones sang in the Lincoln Center's Philharmonic Hall, Mayor John Lindsay proclaimed it "Country Music Day" in New York City. "Country music and New York may not only go together," a newspaper account of the occasion said; "New York may need country music more than country music needs New York."

When the Country Music Association's board was at the Plaza, more than 500 people—most of them Madison Avenue advertising agency executives and media representatives— were treated to a three-hour hoedown under the crystal chandeliers of the Grand Ballroom. "I think it's very refreshing to see this coming in," one guest enthused. "In the fifties and sixties, rock and roll rolled over the country, getting more and more raucous as it went along, especially when the drug aspects got into it. Now there's a swing over to the simple, to the clean, to the healthy. Country music celebrates the goodness of America, faith in America, patriotism." And another, a man whose booking agency, said the New York *Times,* is "not known for its naïveté in the mass-entertainment field," said he thought "the public today is really groping for a new sound, which we haven't had since rock and roll. This could be it."

From the opposite direction—the classics, the so-called serious music—comes the opinion of at least one veteran critic that country and other forms of popular music are so ascendant that classical music will be dead in another fifty years. Henry Pleasants, a native of Philadelphia who has been reviewing symphonic and operatic performances in Europe for the past thirty years, nourishes an open admiration for American jazz and country music, and because he takes them seriously, he is a controversial figure among "serious" music critics.

But Pleasants, and the audiences at the Plaza and the Philharmonic, apparently know which way the wind is blowing. New York used to be the center of the music world and of the recording industry; now the business has gone to Los Angeles and London and most of all to the South, to Nashville and Atlanta and Memphis and Macon and Muscle Shoals, a north Alabama town of 4,000 people. Bill Williams, the country music editor of *Billboard* magazine, estimates that the recording industry in Nashville alone is a $225-million-a-year business—fully one-fourth of the industry's annual gross worldwide—and that the other Southern cities share another one-fourth or more among them. The Southern half of the pie is more than just country music—it's also rhythm and blues, soul, rock, pop, everything but classical. Recording artists as diverse as Perry Como, Joan Baez, Bob Dylan, and the Nitty Gritty Dirt Band are attracted to Nashville by something mystical and evanescent called "the Nashville Sound," an indefinable quality that derives from unexcelled recording studios, superb backup musicians, a cadre of highly professional songwriters and producers and publishers, and an atmosphere that is relaxed and unhurried. "It's a basic style," says Williams. "I can't describe it, but I know it when I hear it. It's been an elixir for a lot of artists, and their coming here has been a real shot in the arm for Nashville."

Most of the more than 300 recording artists who live in and around Nashville are country musicians. Not a few of them are now rich and famous—Grand Ole Opry stars, performers whose records sell millions of copies and whose public appearances are in great demand, musicians with their own syndicated television shows (also made in Nashville). Many of the most successful artists spend most of their time on the road, traveling over the country in customized buses, making one-night stands. It is a hard grind, but highly rewarding. Nobody knows exactly how many millionaires the country music business has made, but the number is high enough to attract thousands of aspiring musicians to Music City, and only a few of them break into the charmed circle.

Country music at its best is down-to-earth, direct, storytelling music. It is about the everyday experiences of ordinary people, about love and faith, playing and praying, working and drinking, living and dying. Down through the years it has been played and sung primarily by and for rural whites who know what poverty is. Of late, its complexion has changed ever so slightly: One of its superstars is a black singer named Charley Pride, and Ray Charles has recorded a double album of country classics, and a few younger performers in the field are black. There is an occasional scattering of blacks in the weekend crowds at the Opry—where, ironically, the first musician to perform almost fifty years ago was a black harmonica player named DeFord Bailey. Pride's blackness is a pigment of the imagination—his style is pure country, not blues or soul—and he has made himself a wealthy man. There is also a popular Mexican American performer, Johnny Davis Rodriguez.

As it has risen in popularity and spread across the country, country music has been modified by new performers, new audiences, and new instruments. The purists, the traditionalists like Roy Acuff and Tex Ritter and Ernest Tubb, are still around and still revered, but they share the stage now with Glen Campbell and Bobby Goldsboro and Kris Kristofferson and Boots Randolph, and the guitars and fiddles have been augmented by electrified instruments and drums and brass and soft strings. The lines that separate country from pop and rock are not always clearly drawn, and as country goes more and more to the city, there is about it a little less twang and a little more slickness. "The music has been increasingly adapted to urban ears," said a story in the New York *Times*. "It has been smoothed out, made more commercially palatable, reduced in twanginess and sometimes crossed with other musical strains to create a contemporary or 'modern' country music sound. . . . The word Western was dropped from the descriptive name 'country and Western' music to reduce its regional identification, and in some places the term 'country' is being dropped in favor of the inclusive designation 'all-American music.' "

In that process of homogenization, country music is finding acceptance and success and affluence such as it has never known. It is a gold mine with a seemingly endless vein, and it is attracting prospectors from every corner of the entertainment world. To many people, it is all too good to be true—if America is looking for a new sound to take the place of rock, and if country is going to be it, this could be the beginning of boom time. But there are others in the field who see something vaguely disquieting in the phenomenon of "modernization." One of the most distinctive things about country music has been the closeness that has existed between the pickers and singers and their audiences. They have shared an intimacy in the music because they also shared a personal knowledge of the experiences it described—poverty and loneliness and all the rest. How much of that intimacy, that authenticity, can be retained when the music goes uptown? When the artists leave the country, when poverty becomes an abstraction in a forgotten past, when the stars live in mansions and drive Cadillacs and belong to the country club—when they are no longer having the experiences they have always sung about—what will it do to the music? And when it is being packaged on

Madison Avenue as "all-American music," will it still be country?

Maybe it won't matter. Maybe the best of the musicians will be able to remember what it was like and keep it honest. Or maybe the fans won't care. They keep flocking in undiminished hordes to Nashville to attend the Opry (which, incidentally, is moving out of its ancient holy temple, the Ryman Auditorium, and into a spanking new structure at Opryland, one of the theme parks inspired by Disneyland), and they ride tour buses on Saturday mornings to see the homes of the stars, just like in Hollywood, and they go to the Country Music Hall of Fame on what is called Music Row to look at the old guitars under glass, and the gold records, and all the artifacts of the good old days, and for many of them, it is an unforgettable experience. They will surely keep on coming.

But country music is outgrowing that simple style. It is going big-time, getting into TV specials and advertising contracts and dozens of avenues to wealth. It is putting its slick boot forward, the one without the dust and cow dung on it. The other boot may survive only in the museum, along with the old fiddles and guitars and cowboy hats. Country music, and the people in it, and the people around it, have survived some hard times. Now the test is to see whether they can survive the good times.

In H. L. Mencken's day, culture was seen as something to be reserved for refined and sophisticated people; it had nothing to do with the "crude masses," who were supposedly lacking in "cultivation" and the "finer qualities." In a curious and ironic way, Mencken—the iconoclast, the debunker, the acerbic critic—supported that attitude of haughty elitism. The "American *Kultur*" he castigated the South for lacking in "The Sahara of the Bozart" was high culture—formal, serious, exclusive. It was a standard of quality, taste, and style defined and certified by "experts" and "masters."

That sort of narrow and restricted view of culture no longer dominates American life. There is more latitude and diversity in style and taste and fashion now, and culture is more broadly understood and applied to encompass the lives and interests and endeavors of all people, rather than the pursuits of an elite minority.

Two conflicting and contradictory pressures now influence the shape and substance of culture in the United States, pulling it toward opposite poles. The first is a sort of neoelitism, a fragmentation and splintering of life styles into separate packages that seldom breach the walls dividing them. The vestiges of high culture fit comfortably in that mold, but so do religious cults and communes and suburban walled communities and a great many other self-contained and restricted groups defined by race or sex or age or ideology. Tom Wolfe described the phenomenon in his book *The Pump House Gang;* the esoteric "statuspheres" he wrote about—the surfers, the motorcyclists, the swinging singles—define themselves by their differences. They are, in their own separate ways, elite, exclusive, isolated—they conform to a narrow code, and they are often hostile and suspicious of all that lies outside their sphere.

The other major pressure that is shaping American culture is essentially assimilationist. It is the pressure of homogenization, the force that causes Disneyland to spawn dozens of imitators and country music to be pasteurized to suit the tastes of a wider audience. Television is its ultimate instrument. The impulse to corner the market, to absorb and coopt and swallow up everything, and then to spew it back as "novelty," not only caters to prevalent tastes and fashions—it also creates demand by artificial stimulation.

The South, no less than the nation as a whole, is under the influence of neoelitism and assimilation, being pulled both toward fragmentation and toward homogenization. If there is a middle ground, an integration of cultures that thrives on both unity and diversity, that exalts both relationships and differences, it is not very much in evidence.

Epilogue

Headed south on Amtrak's *Floridian:*

Union Station in Nashville is a Gothic memorial to a bygone day, a fortress of towers and arches and peaked roofs and chimneys. Its limestone façade is stained with soot, and grass grows in its lofty gutters. Inside, under a massive arched ceiling of stained glass squares, there is a treasure trove of hand-finished craftsmanship—mahogany and marble and tile and more stained glass, bas-relief murals, sculpted and painted angels and robed maidens, an antique clock running an hour late.

There are no people, and it is cool and deathly quiet, like a church. In one corner, a neon sign that says TICKET OFFICE glows above a glass door. The lone agent is courteous and patient. The *Floridian,* he says, leaves Nashville at 9:05 A.M. and arrives in Montgomery at 3:45 P.M. The fare is $11.50, one way. The train begins in Chicago each evening and arrives

209

in Miami about forty hours later. Going South through Nashville, it has been averaging about 130 passengers; on the return North, the average is higher—about 150.

A notice taped to the agent's window says that as of August 2, 1973, the *Floridian* will be discontinued. It is the last passenger train still running on the Chicago-Louisville-Nashville-Birmingham-Miami route.

I rode a train to Chicago once, with my mother and my brother and my two sisters. I was nine. It was high adventure. The silverware in the dining car was rich-looking, heavy. They had tongue sandwiches. The waiters didn't smile.

The train pulls in on time—three coach cars, a pullman, and a dining car behind a humming diesel and a baggage car. The crew is from the L&N; the cars belong to the U.S. Department of Transportation, to Amtrak. "We're making the trains worth traveling again," their brochure says. "Amtrak is setting the stage for a new era in rail transportation." The cars are silver, with red and blue trim. They are relatively new, and reasonably comfortable.

My assigned seat is number 38, next to a woman from Chicago who is just rousing from a restless night. Her hair is in curlers. There had been a mixup on her ticket. "Never again," she vows. "Next time I'll fly."

Seventeen minutes late, we begin to roll—smooth and silent at first, like a boat on water, and then squeak, click, sway. The hot July sun is already baking the streets, but the train is cool and carpeted. We snake past warehouses, and pass beside and then under an interstate highway.

Tom Wicker once wrote a column in the New York Times *about a trip he had made back to the South—he's from North Carolina. He described it as "the new, prosperous, progressive, homogenous South, with its concrete arteries and shrieking jets and piercing neon." Every year, he said, it seems "more nearly an interchangeable part of the vast, grim sameness of a nation that has discovered in mobility that no one need ever*

*leave home because everything and every place can be made to
look, taste, feel and sound like every other thing and place."
He said a new architectural style—Airport Modern—is now as
commonplace as the Railroad Gothic of a half-century ago, and
the car you rent with your credit card at the airport takes you
along the same commercial strip to the same chain motel and
restaurant, whether you happen to be in Montgomery or Little
Rock or Indianapolis or Sacramento.*

A black man across the aisle keeps staring at a young white
man with long hair who is standing up a few seats away.
Finally he calls to him: "You watch *Roller Derby?* You look
just like Ronnie Raines." "Yeah, I watch it," the young man
answers, smiling shyly. "But I ain't him."

Pop, snap, rumble, jostle, jerk. Picking up speed, still
hugging the interstate. And then, into a limestone canyon and
out into suburbia, dewy and pastoral-looking. A shopping
center. Riding mowers, minibikes, boats and trailers in the
backyards, new houses under construction.

*The blunt instruments of homogenization—automobiles,
television, computers, credit cards—are double-sided devices;
they liberate, and they imprison. We have mobility, and
money (or credit), and at least the appearance of choices, so
we move and spend and choose: new cars come in infinite
combinations of color and style and "extras," a beckoning
multiplicity of motels and restaurants and "attractions" com-
petes for the traveling trade, a dizzying array of packaged
goods lines the store shelves. But at bottom it is a bogus
diversity, a choice without a difference. Homogenization is
rampant on the American landscape, and the assault on the
senses accumulates and overwhelms and stultifies: plastic
glasses under a membrane of Saran Wrap, Athens in ruins on
the vinyl wallpaper, 100 million vehicles on the road, 200,000
service stations pumping 100 billion gallons of gas a year.
Gargantuan shopping malls with postage-stamp parking lots,
architectural atrocities of prefabrication, high-rise "homes"*

for the elderly, organized orgies for swinging singles, Johnny Carson making tired wisecracks in living color on the ubiquitous tube, McDonald's hamburger number 13 billion-plus. Dial 9 for outside and 8 for long distance. Recorded telephone messages, electronic signature scanners, computerized billing, plastic flowers, instant food, massage parlors, chic-porn, acronyms, security guards, drive-in churches, artificial lakes, terminal degrees. There is one face on America, and it is gigantic, stretching from Miami to Boston to Seattle to San Diego.

There is a little boy in front of me, riding with his mother. He is corpulent and verbose and wiggly. "I'm sick," he says. "I didn't sleep all night." His name is Garrett. He is seven. The conductor, a rotund, graying, bespectacled man who looks like Harry Golden, stops by the boy's seat. "You look healthy to me," he says. "Just keep breathing." He laughs, and strikes a mock blow on Garrett's chubby shoulder.

When I was about sixteen, I rode a train from Washington to Cincinnati, and sat up all night smooching with a girl from Texarkana. She was a little bit skinny, and had blond hair.

Finally, thirty minutes out of the station, we are in the country: hazy blue hills in the distance, farmhouses under maple shade, white fences and gravel lanes, cattle grazing. *I know a lady who speaks proudly of her "black anguish" cattle.* Corn fields and tobacco patches, ponds reflecting trees and sky. No billboards.

The land of grace and violence, of King Cotton and legalized segregation, of one-party politics and religious piety and cultural isolation and rural simplicity—that land is almost gone. Call it what you will—the New South, the Contemporary South, the Maturing South—something different is emerging now. Cities are rising, industry is booming, universities are gaining size and strength, Space Age technology is spreading, tourists and new residents are flowing in. There is some evidence of increasing moderation in race relations, and of less desperate circumstance for the poor—in some places, anyway. In a relative sense, at least, things are better than they used to be for the people of the South, and there is a lot of talk about a new image.

We are passing in and out of little towns, and their main streets look like movie sets. The flag flies in front of the post office, the regulars sit on benches on the courthouse lawn. The towns have subdivisions of their own, just like the cities, and they have slums, miniature ghettos with unwritten names like Lickskillet and Niggertown.

Sometimes the little towns are the least changed, but not always. In some places, school desegregation has been remarkably successful. But the crippling strain of race and class prejudice persists. It takes different forms, but it is there, in the towns and in the cities. In the contemporary South, race is yet another issue—like urbanization and politics and industrialization and the rest—that has assumed a national character, and national dimensions. The civil rights movement ushered in the Second Reconstruction, and the South was divested of the one characteristic that most clearly separated it from the rest of the nation: legalized segregation and white supremacy. Now the post-Reconstruction era has arrived, and privilege based on race and class permeates the total society, North as well as South. The American white majority, the affluent majority, does not believe in equality and an open society.

There are about 150 people on the train—most of them in the coach cars—and about half of them are black. One of the cars has an observation deck, a glass-enclosed bubble with twenty-four seats. The kids have discovered it, and they are playing up there.

"Get your black hands off my sandals!" a little girl shouts.

"Shut your mouth, white girl!" the boy replies. They both giggle.

We have slowed down. Passing between the cars, I can

hear birds singing, and the hiss of the brakes, and I can smell tar and creosote. The whistle blows. It lacks something— mournfulness, maybe. It somehow sounds too efficient, too impersonal. We pass a pile of junked refrigerators and stoves.

Consumption is what it's all about—that and success. It all goes together—the striving, the competing, the acquiring. The goal is to get to the top, to win, to be Number One. No substitute for victory, whether the subject is wealth or war or fame or games or souls. So we have walled communities and selective schools and exclusive churches and private clubs and the Green Berets and the Junior League and Sigma Chi and Chi Omega and Hilton Head and Playboy Clubs and Shriners and black separatism and Hell's Angels and the drug culture. Everybody has to be somewhere, and be somebody. Fragmentation— homogenization's counterpoint. We are the same, and different. We can't reconcile equality and diversity, so we settle for being homogenized and fragmented.

We are passing through Decatur, crossing the Tennessee River. A motor boat pulling a water skier passes soundlessly beneath us. Up in the bubble top, Garrett is romping with a newfound friend. He seems fully recovered. He is wearing a button the conductor gave him. It says TRACKS ARE BACK.

George Wallace and Ted Kennedy met in Decatur on the Fourth of July. It was billed as a Democratic summit meeting, and it was a love feast. Some supporters and enemies of both men didn't like it. Wallace's mail was mostly critical, and Kennedy's press was mixed at best. Some blacks smelled a honkie in the woodpile. Would the two of them dare to put a ticket together? Sure. Politics is compromise, not ideology.

Back at my seat, my companion has taken down her hair, and her temper is improved. She is pleasant to talk to. She is going to visit her mother in St. Petersburg. Out the window, the kudzu and honeysuckle and pine thickets have reappeared. It's almost time for lunch. We are near an interstate highway again, and a Holiday Inn billboard comes into view. *"Man is born free, and everywhere he is in chains." Rousseau said it. It could be Holiday Inn's motto.*

In the dining car, the menu has Welsh rarebit, beefsteak and mushroom pie, sandwiches. The waiters are taciturn and abrupt, and their eyes speak volumes. They ride from Chicago to Miami. The conductor and the engineer are relieved in Birmingham.

And Birmingham is coming up; we are already passing scrap metal heaps, junked car graveyards, gray and grimy furnaces, warehouses, smokestacks.

"Momma, I've gotta throw up." It's Garrett again. The statue of Vulcan is barely visible in the distance, all but obliterated by the haze. The sun is a dull gray disk, and it makes shimmering mirages of water on the streets.

"What happens when you flush in the station?"

"I don't know. Get out and see."

The train is motionless for what seems like a long time. Finally, thirty minutes behind schedule, we begin to roll again.

The swelling of the cities seems unstoppable. The poor come in from the country, hoping they can find what is no longer available to them anywhere else: work, a living. The affluent get uptight about having so many poor people and black people and "different" people around them, so they flee to the country. They're just swapping places, passing like ships in the night. The vital organs of the city decay, so they are eviscerated by urban renewal, and slum housing is replaced by skyscrapers and freeways, and the poor are made mobile again. That's part of the New South too, the New Union. There is plenty of mobility—too much—and not all of it is voluntary, or upward.

A young woman with sandy hair and freckles is sitting two seats forward. She is reading a Russian novel.

"Is that a good book?" I ask her.

"Oh, yes, it's very good." She is a secretary and bookkeeper for a feed mill in Nashville. She has finished college, but a year ago she started taking Russian, "just for the stimulation." Now she talks about applying for a fellowship to study for a year in Moscow. She is going to Montgomery to visit her sister. While we chat, I hear another conversation heating up:

"Nixon's in the hospital on a sympathy kick. I think he planned the whole Watergate plot, and now he's trying to weasel out of it."

"That's cruel. You think he's lying about everything. Even about being sick. Why do you blame everything on him?"

We are too shellshocked to be outraged anymore. Assassinations and riots and Vietnam and the campus revolts and the drug scene and crime in the streets and crime in the corporations and crime in the government are just too much to grasp. It takes no nostalgic longing for "the good old days," no disdain for "progress," no pessimistic nature, to see a tragedy of historic proportions gathering on the horizon. The America of righteousness and certitude and invincibility is up against some problems that don't have ready solutions and questions that don't have easy answers.

The bubble top is quiet now, almost empty. A black man with a bushy mustache and his head shaved is sitting in the rear. I sit down across the aisle from him, and directly he asks me for a light.

"Where you goin'?" he says.

"Montgomery."

"Me too. Goin' to Tuskegee, actually. If I can catch me a bus."

"Is that your home?"

"Yeah. I work in Chicago. I'm just goin' back to visit some of my people. Five more years, though, and I'll be goin' back for good."

"How long you been livin' in Chicago?"

"I been there twenty-five years. Chicago ain't where I live, though. It's where I stay. Chicago's *existin'*. Tuskegee is *livin'*." He looks at me and smiles.

At mid-afternoon it is quiet in the coach, and the sun is warm through the window. The train thumps and grunts and bounces, and the movement becomes almost rhythmic, mesmerizing. There must be thousands of freight cars rusting in the weeds on the sidings. Siluria, Calera, Jemison, Thorsby, Clanton, the little towns blur past. Drowsiness is irresistible.

"All that stuff you say about equality is a bunch of crap," Bill Robertson said. "You're just crazy as hell. But I don't hold it against you. You're my friend, and I value your friendship too much to let that stand between us. So I just ignore it. It's just as if you had a tic, or a harelip. I just pretend it isn't there."

Garrett is awake and playing again, talking rapidly in his Chicago accent. "You look like you're colored," he says to a black kid, touching him cautiously on the head.

"I *am* colored, you dope. You ain't *nothin'*."

A little girl with blond pigtails and an Alabama drawl says to Garrett: "It doesn't matter, just so long as you're a person." A spirited game of tag ensues.

So much has changed, and for the better. And so much hasn't, and probably won't. And a lot has changed for the worse. We're losing what's worth keeping, and spreading what we ought to lose, and keeping some bad qualities, even learning some new ones. What's going to become of kinship and closeness and family reunions, and manners and politeness and common courtesy, and pit barbecue and country ham and smoked sausage and fried catfish and homemade peach ice cream?

"Montgomery," the conductor says. "Montgomery, Alabama."

The people are gone from the Land Between the Rivers. Whites are leaving the public schools of Atlanta, being replaced by the black and white poor, by people from places like Luverne, Alabama. The New Carpetbaggers have come to Plainville, and to scores of other towns and cities. Were it not for Watergate, there would be a New American Majority aligned with Richard Nixon—and there may yet be one, loyal to George Wallace or John Connally or Teddy Kennedy. Southern cities have all the symptoms of the diseases that imperil the cities of the North. There is a New Evangelism, and a New Disney World of Fantasy, and if Madison Avenue buys it, there will be a New American Music.

Outside the station, a man passing by in his car stops in the middle of the street and rolls down the window. "Did a passenger train just come in here? Well, I'll be damned. I didn't even know there still *was* one. They don't advertise it or anything. Some of my family just went off to Chicago on the bus last week. And they coulda rode the train."

The man with the bald head and the mustache stands on the curb, suitcase in one hand, a cardboard box in the other. He looks up at the thunderclouds blowing easterly in a sultry breeze. Then he starts up the street toward the bus station.

Index

Aaron, Hank, 181
Abernathy, Ralph David, 3
Acuff, Roy, 202, 206
Agrarians, 15–16, 108
Agribusiness conglomerates, 28,
  30, 33, 38, 47
Agricultural cooperatives, 28
Agriculture, 26–47
Agriculture, U.S. Department of,
  30, 50, 53
Alger, Horatio, 180
Ali, Muhammad, 181
Allen University, 164
Allman Brothers, 202
American Civil Liberties Union,
  92
American Friends Service Com-
  mittee, 158, 160

American Indians, 48, 50, 53, 57,
  182
American Report, 194
Appalachia, 55, 56–57
Appalachian Regional Commis-
  sion, 57
Armageddon Experience, 193
Armstrong, Louis, 202
Arnall, Ellis, 7
Ashmore, Harry, 3
Askew, Reubin, 1, 10–11, 13, 102–
  103, 148
Athletics, 176–181
Atkins, Chet, 202
Atlanta, Georgia, 89–93
"Atlanta Compromise," 92
Atlanta *Constitution*, 90
Atlanta *Journal*, 90
Atwood, George Conroy, 71–72

219

Grady, Henry, 1–16, 92, 106, 108
Graham, Billy, 138, 192–196, 198, 200
Graham, Hugh Davis, 131–132
Grand Ole Opry, 203, 205, 207
Grange, The, 32
Grantham, Dewey, 5
Greater Columbia Chamber of Commerce, 153, 165
Greene County, Alabama, 148
Greenville, South Carolina, 85–89
Greider, William, 70
Gunther, John, 185
Guthrie, Woody, 185

Haggard, Merle, 138
Hall, J. Floyd, 87–89
Hall, Roger Griffin, 175
Hamer, Fannie Lou, 3
Handy, W. C., 202
Harbison, South Carolina, 165–167, 171
Harding, Vincent, 3
Harrill, Ernest, 87–88
Harris, Fred, 149
Harris, Louis, 171
Hayes, Isaac, 202
Hayes, Rutherford B., 23, 147
Haynsworth, Clement F., Jr., 85, 137
Hays, Brooks, 136
Health, Education, and Welfare, Department of, 95
Henderson, Vivian, 3
Highlander Research and Education Center, 183
Holton, Linwood, 148
Housing and Urban Development, U.S. Department of, 165
Huge, Harry, 146
Humphrey, Hubert, 129, 130

Indian Affairs, Bureau of, 50, 53
Industry, 104–125
Innis, Roy, 139

Installment land sale business, 53–55
Interior, U.S. Department of the, 50
International Festival of Country Music, 203
International Student Congress on Evangelism, 193
International Telephone & Telegraph Corporation, 53

Jenkins, Casey, 95, 96
Jenkins, Lincoln, 159, 163
Jesus freaks, 192–194
Jesus Sound Explosion, 193
Johnson, Lyndon B., 15, 77, 130, 133–135, 138–140, 149
Jones, Ashton, 186
Jones, Bob, 195
Jones, George, 203
Jones, Norman E., 144
Joplin, Janis, 202
Jordan, Barbara, 12, 132–133, 146, 149
Jordan, Clarence, 186–187
Jordan, Vernon, 3
Justice, U.S. Department of, 96, 97

Kefauver, Estes, 135
Kelly, William, 68
Kennedy, Edward M., 39, 214, 218
Kennedy, John F., 61, 77
Kennedy, Robert F., 143
Kentucky Dam, 61
Kerouac, Jack, 185
Kerr-McGee Oil Company, 65
King, Martin Luther, Jr., 143
Kirk, Claude, 13
Kitchens, Claud, 163
Kohlmeier, Louis M., 137
Koinonia Farm, Americus, Ga., 186–187, 191
Kolb, James, 39–43, 46

DATE DUE
